Lecture Notes of the Institute for Computer Sciences, Social Informatics and Telecommunications Engineering 437

More information about this series at https://link.springer.com/bookseries/8197

Kaishun Wu · Lu Wang · Yanjiao Chen (Eds.)

Edge Computing and IoT: Systems, Management and Security

Second EAI International Conference, ICECI 2021
Virtual Event, December 22–23, 2021
Proceedings

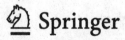 Springer

Editors
Kaishun Wu (iD)
Shenzhen University
Shenzhen, China

Lu Wang (iD)
Shenzhen University
Shenzhen, China

Yanjiao Chen
Zhejiang University
Huangzhou, China

ISSN 1867-8211   ISSN 1867-822X (electronic)
Lecture Notes of the Institute for Computer Sciences, Social Informatics
and Telecommunications Engineering
ISBN 978-3-031-04230-0   ISBN 978-3-031-04231-7 (eBook)
https://doi.org/10.1007/978-3-031-04231-7

This Springer imprint is published by the registered company Springer Nature Switzerland AG
The registered company address is: Gewerbestrasse 11, 6330 Cham, Switzerland

Preface

We are delighted to introduce the proceedings of the second edition of the European Alliance for Innovation (EAI) International Conference on Edge Computing and IoT: Systems, Management and Security (ICECI 2021). This conference aims to bring together computer scientists, industrial engineers, and researchers to discuss and exchange experimental or theoretical results, novel designs, work-in-progress, experience, case studies, and trend-setting ideas in the area of edge computing or IoT including all aspects with emphasis on systems, management, and security.

The technical program of ICECI 2021 consisted of 12 full papers at the main conference tracks: Track 1 - Edge Computing and Track 2 - Internet of Things. Aside from the high-quality technical paper presentations, the technical program also featured two keynote speeches and three tutorials. The two keynote speeches were given by Wei Zhao from the Shenzhen Institute of Advanced Technology and Qian Zhang from the Hong Kong University of Science and Technology. The three tutorials were presented by Jin Zhang from the Southern University of Science and Technology, Jiliang Wang from Tsinghua University, and Yanjiao Chen from Zhejiang University.

Coordination with the steering chair, Imrich Chlamtac, was essential for the success of the conference. We sincerely appreciate his constant support and guidance. It was also a great pleasure to work with such an excellent organizing committee team for their hard work in organizing and supporting the conference. In particular, we are grateful to the Technical Program Committee, who completed the peer-review process for the technical papers and helped to put together a high-quality technical program. We are also grateful to Conference Manager Rupali Tiwari for her support and all the authors who submitted their papers to the ICECI 2021 conference and workshops.

We strongly believe that the ICECI conference provides a good forum for all researchers, developers, and practitioners to discuss all science and technology aspects that are relevant to edge computing and IoT. We also expect that the future ICECI conferences will be as successful and stimulating as this year's, as indicated by the contributions presented in this volume.

Kaishun Wu
Lu Wang
Yanjiao Chen

Organization

Steering Committee

Imrich Chlamtac — University of Trento, Italy

Organizing Committee

General Chair

Kaishun Wu — Shenzhen University, China

Technical Program Committee Chairs and Co-chairs

Lu Wang — Shenzhen University, China
Yanjiao Chen — Zhejiang University, China

Sponsorship and Exhibit Chair

Jian Zhang — Wuhan University, China

Local Chairs

Haodi Zhang — Shenzhen University, China
Yongpan Zou — Shenzhen University, China
Zhidan Liu — Shenzhen University, China

Workshops Chair

Ting Wang — East China Normal University, China

Publicity and Social Media Chairs

Dian Zhang — Lingnan University, Hong Kong
Jin Zhang — Southern University of Science and Technology, China

Publications Chair

Dandan Liu — Wuhan University, China

Web Chairs

Jiang Xiao   Huazhong University of Science and Technology,
                                China

Zhice Yang   ShanghaiTech University, China

Technical Program Committee

Hongliang Bi   Northwestern Polytechnical University, China
Chu Cao   Nanyang Technological University, Singapore
Li Chen   University of Louisiana at Lafayette, USA
Yan Chen   University of Science and Technology of China,
                                China
Qianyi Huang   Southern University of Science and Technology,
                                China
Feng Liu   Shenzhen University, China
Gang Liu   Nokia Shanghai Bell, China
Xiaoke Qi   China University of Political Science and Law,
                                China
Yuanfeng Song   WeBank, China
Panrong Tong   Nanyang Technological University, Singapore
Liyao Xiang   Shanghai Jiao Tong University, China
Yang Yang   Zhongnan University of Economics and Law,
                                China
Xiaoyan Yin   Northwestern University, China
Xu Yuan   University of Louisiana at Lafayette, USA

Contents

Edge Computing

An Improved Audio Processing Method for Campus Broadcast System

Xueying Li[1], Bo Liu[1,2(✉)], and Haoyu Zhou[1,2]

[1] College of Information and Intelligent Science and Technology, Hunan Agricultural University, Changsha 410128, China
6633873@qq.com
[2] Hunan Engineering Research Center of Agricultural and Rural Information, Changsha 410128, China

Abstract. A campus broadcast system is an important tool for school teaching and propaganda. However, different classrooms need to broadcast in separate channels decentralization and time-sharing at the same time, so it leads to more transmitted signals, frequent data interaction, bandwidth consumption, often large information delay, intermittent voice, and poor user experience. In order to reduce bandwidth and sampling frequency, based on compressed sensing theory, this paper proposes an optimized regular orthogonal matching tracking algorithm for audio processing (OROMP). This algorithm uses discrete wavelet transform as a sparse basis and the audio signal is sampled by Gaussian random matrix, then the optimized ROMP algorithm is used for audio reconstruction to improve the sound quality and precision of speech signal reconstruction in the broadcasting system. When the load of the broadcast terminal is less than 200 and the maximum shunting is 30, the audio delay time can be controlled below 200 ms, the residual error is about 1/4 of the OMP algorithm. The reconstruction time is reduced and the reconstruction quality is improved, which can meet the normal use of a large campus.

Keywords: Audio compressed sensing · Optimized regular orthogonal matching pursuit algorithm · Audio signal · The campus broadcast

1 Introduction

In the face of massive data and ultra-high transmission rate of the information age, the traditional Nyquist-Shannon sampling theorem is inadequate, and compressed sensing theory is put forward, just to solve the data redundancy, the waste of computing resources and storage resources, and the burden of data processing and transmission. The theoretical breakthrough was proposed by mathematicians Tao, Rom berg, and Donoho by around 2005 [1, 2]. Then, the researchers further supplemented the mathematical basis of compressed sensing theory and gave some theoretical analysis results [3–5]. Since then, compressed sensing theory has been widely used in many projects [6–8], especially in audio processing, a series of solutions are proposed [9–14].

K. Wu et al. (Eds.): ICECI 2021, LNICST 437, pp. 3–12, 2022.
https://doi.org/10.1007/978-3-031-04231-7_1

With the development of network technology and audio technology, IP network broadcasting applications emerge. Nowadays, campus broadcasting begins to use the digital network for broadcasting. Compared with an analog channel, network transmission not only solves the problem of channel monopoly but also better solves the problems of sound quality loss and multi-channel cross-transmission. However, new challenges arise, such as grouping, decentralization, time-sharing and random broadcasting of different classrooms, which leads to too many transmitted signals, frequent data upload and download interactions, and too much bandwidth occupation, resulting in large digital transmission delay, intermittent voice and poor user experience. In order to solve the above problems, this paper proposes a compressed sensing audio processing method for campus broadcast based on an optimized regular orthogonal matching pursuit algorithm.

2 Audio Compressed Sensing

The core idea of audio compressed sensing is to randomly sample signals with a density sparser than Nyquist sampling frequency, which can compress signals and restore original signals with a better method. Therefore, audio compressed sensing focuses on three aspects: sparse basis, observation matrix, and reconstruction algorithm. Audio compression sensing technology will be described in three parts below.

2.1 The Sparse Matrix

One of the preconditions to realize compressed sensing is that the signal satisfies sparsity in the frequency domain. The purpose of signal sparse representation is to represent the signal as completely as possible in the transform domain with as few atoms as possible. It makes the signal more compact and easier to obtain the main information of the signal [9]. If the number of non-zero points of the signal in a certain domain is far less than the total number of signal points, the signal is sparse in that domain. For compressed sensing, as long as the signal is approximately sparse in a certain transform domain.

If the compression technology is applied to the field of audio processing, it is necessary to find the sparse basis of audio signal processing. For example, Candes, etc. [10] proposed the sparse representation of speech signal in discrete cosine transform domain; Y. Gao etc. [11] used wavelet transforms to sparse represent speech signal; W.Derouaz etc. [12] used k-singular value decomposition algorithm to sparse represent a signal. S. Sahu etc. [13] DWT can bring better sparse performance and further improve reconstruction performance compared with other sparse matrices according to the measurement indexes.

2.2 Observation Matrix

Through the observation matrix Φ, the signal can be reduced from n dimension to m dimension (M ≪ N). Tao and Candes proved that Restricted isometric Property (RIP) is an accurate requirement for an observational matrix [1]. However, it is very complicated to determine whether a matrix satisfies RIP. Therefore, Baraniuk [15] proved that the equivalent condition for RIP is that the observational matrix and sparse representation basis are unrelated. Definition of correlation:

$$\mu(\Phi, \Psi) = \sqrt{n} \cdot \max_{1 \leq k, j \leq n} |\langle \varphi_k, \psi_j \rangle| \tag{1}$$

where φ_k, ψ_j are the row vectors and column vectors of the matrix Φ and Ψ respectively. According to Eq. (1), the smaller μ is, the less relevant Φ and Ψ are. At present, the commonly used random observation matrices include random Gaussian observation matrix, random Benoulli observation matrix, and row step observation matrix.

2.3 Reconstruction Algorithm

On the premise that the sampling matrix satisfies the RIP condition, the signal is sufficiently sparse and the compression rate is appropriate, the sampling process can capture almost all the information of the sparse component of the original signal, and the sparse coefficient θ is solved by an infinite number of solutions. According to the sparse condition, the solution with the least non-zero elements can be picked out from all feasible solutions, which is the solution with the most sparsity. Considering the noise, formulation (2) can be obtained:

$$\min \|x\|_0 \text{ s.t. } \|Ax - y\|_2^2 \leq \varepsilon \tag{2}$$

Zero norm constraint in the objective function is an NP-hard problem, so Tao proved that under certain conditions, the zero-norm problem is equivalent to the one norm problem, so the above model is transformed into a formulation (3):

$$\min \|x\|_1 \text{ s.t. } \|Ax - y\|_2^2 \leq \varepsilon \tag{3}$$

The core problem of compressed sensing theory in signal reconstruction. The existing reconstruction algorithms are mainly divided into Convex Relaxation (CR) algorithm, Greedy algorithm (GIA), I_P optimization algorithm and combination algorithm [16].

3 Audio Processing Methods

If x is the campus broadcast a continuous audio signal collected, $x = [x(1), x(2), \cdots, x(N)]^T \in R^{(N \times 1)}$. Ψ as matrix, θ is the n-dimensional vector sparse coefficient, $x = \Psi\theta$.

3.1 Sparse Representation of Audio Signals in DWT

When sparse representation of audio is used, different sparse bases can make audio signals have different sparsity. At present, most of the sparse bases are orthogonal matrices. The commonly used sparse bases of audio compressed sensing are discrete cosine transform (DCT), discrete Fourier transform (DFT), discrete wavelet transform (DWT), Kanade-Lucas-Tomasi (KLT) and so on. In this paper, DWT is used to sparse represent the audio signal collected by campus broadcast.

As shown in Fig. 1, discrete wavelet transforms process diagram, the discrete input signal $f_u^{(i)}$, passing through low-pass filter u and high pass filter v respectively, and then

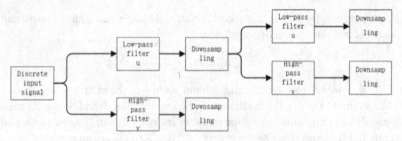

Fig. 1. Process diagram of discrete wavelet transform

through down sampling filter, the approximate coefficient of low-pass filter-branch is obtained $f_u^{(i+1)}$, the high pass filter-branch obtains the detail coefficient $f_v^{(i+1)}$. Wavelet analysis provides approximate coefficients and detail coefficients. The low-frequency information of the signal is given by approximation, and the high-frequency information is given by detail coefficients. Because the low-frequency signal is more important than the high-frequency signal, the output of the low-pass filter is used as the input of the next decomposition stage, while the output of the high-pass filter is used in signal reconstruction. The calculation of wavelet coefficient adopts the method of sequence filtering and down-sampling, and the formula corresponds to (4) and (5).

$$f_u^{(i)}(j) = \sum_{k=1}^{2^{n-i+1}} u(k - 2j)f_u^{(i-1)}(k) \ j = 1, 2, \ldots, 2^{n-i} \tag{4}$$

$$f_v^{(i)}(j) = \sum_{k=1}^{2^{n-i+1}} v(k - 2j)f_v^{(i-1)}(k) \ j = 1, 2, \ldots, 2^{n-i} \tag{5}$$

3.2 Signal Reconstruction

Reconstruction is an inverse process of compression, whose goal is to use fewer observations and relatively small algorithm overhead to obtain reconstructed speech that meets the needs of human auditory perception [5]. The existing reconstruction algorithms can be divided into three categories.

The first is the greedy iterative algorithm, which is proposed for the combinatorial optimization problem. This kind of algorithm mainly takes the relationship between signal and Atomic Dictionary as a way to measure atoms (coefficients) more effectively or non-zero. The basic principle is to find the support set of sparse vectors iteratively and use the constrained support least squares estimation to reconstruct the signal. MP algorithm selects the column with the largest residual inner product of the signal from the measurement matrix at each iteration to construct the sparse approximation of the signal. However, in the MP algorithm, the projection of the measured values in the selected atom set is non-orthogonal, so the approximation obtained in each iteration is suboptimal. The orthogonal matching pursuit (OMP) algorithm developed based on the MP algorithm solves this problem well. ROMP belongs to a kind of bottom-up OMP algorithms. This kind of algorithm uses the atomic selection principle of the MP algorithm to select the atomic update support set and obtains the optimal solution through the least square method. The difference of each algorithm lies in the atomic selection method. ROMP algorithm is shown in Fig. 2:

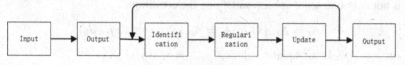

Fig. 2. ROMP flow chart

The second kind is the convex optimization algorithm. The optimization problem satisfying the two conditions that the objective function is a convex function and the feasible set must be a convex set is called convex optimization, that is, the process of finding the global maximum of the convex function on the convex set is called convex optimization. The principle of the convex optimization algorithm is to transform the non-convex reconstruction problem of NP-hard into a convex problem, to reconstruct the original signal by solving the linear programming problem. The most commonly used convex optimization algorithms are the basic pursuit algorithm (BP) and total variation algorithm (TV).

The third is the reconstruction algorithm based on the Bayesian framework. This kind of algorithm considers the time correlation and improves the reconstruction accuracy. Such algorithms include the Expectation - maximization (EM) algorithm, Bayesian Compressive Sensing (BCS) algorithm, Multiple Sparse Bayesian Learning (MSBL) based on Multiple Measurement Vectors (MMV) model, etc.

3.3 OROMP Algorithm

During the reconstruction, if the inner product of the sensing matrix and the allowance are calculated in each iteration, the reconstruction time will increase. The algorithm in this paper only uses the inner product method to calculate the sensing matrix and the allowance in the first iteration, and the inner product calculation is replaced by the subtraction operation of the vector in the subsequent iterations. Therefore, only one inner product operation is needed from the beginning of iteration to the end of the iteration, which reduces the reconstruction time.

The process of the optimized regular orthogonal matching tracking algorithm is as follows:

Input: M * N sensor matrix $A = \Phi\Psi$; N * 1 dimension observation vector y; signal sparsity K.
Output: signal sparse representation coefficient estimation $\hat{\theta}$; N * 1 dimension residuals $r_k = y - A_k\hat{\theta}_k$.
Initialization: $r_0 = y$, $\Lambda_0 = \emptyset$, $A_0 = \emptyset$, $t = 1$.
Repeat the following steps until $r_t = 0$ or t > K or $\|\Lambda_t\|_0 \geq 2K$.
Identification: calculate $u = abs[A^T r_{i-1}]$ and select the K column with the largest absolute value of the inner product. If there are not enough K non-zero values in all the inner products, all the columns with non-zero inner product values are selected and the inner product is selected to the corresponding serial number to form the set J.

Regularization: judge $|u(i)| \leq 2|u(j)|$ for all $i, j \in J_0$, the maximum absolute value of the inner product of each column vector and residuals cannot be more than two times greater than the minimum value and the group with the highest energy is selected because there is not only one set of subsets satisfying the condition.

$$\Lambda_t = \Lambda_{t-1} \cup J_0, A_t = A_{t-1} \cup a_j (\text{for all } j \in J_0)$$

Solution: $y = A_t \theta_t$ Least squares solution: $y_{t+1} = y_t - y_t[J_t]X_{J_t}$
Update: $r_t = y - A_t \hat{\theta}_t, t = t + 1$.

4   Simulation Test

Experimental environment: laptop Dell, Intel Core i7-6700, memory 8 GB, hard disk 256G, Win10 system. The experimental process is shown in Fig. 3:

Fig. 3. ROMP flow chart

Select a signal "1058" collected from the campus broadcast, with a signal length of 22800, Φ is randomly generated during the experiment. The MATLAB simulation signal waveform is shown in Fig. 4. After the original audio signal is transformed by DWT, the approximate coefficients and detail coefficients are shown in Fig. 5.

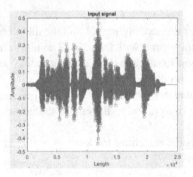

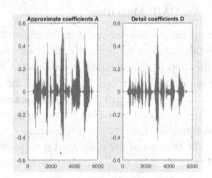

Fig. 4. Speech signal waveform   **Fig. 5.** DWT coefficients

4.1   Reconstruction of Audio Signal by the OROMP Algorithm in DWT Domain

Figure 6 shows the original audio signal is divided into frames, the frame length is 256, and the frame shift is 128. Figure 7 shows the windowed audio signal diagram, and the selected audio signal is added with a Hamming window, as shown in Fig. 8. After MATLAB simulation, the reconstructed signal diagram of the OMP algorithm is shown in Fig. 9, and the reconstructed signal diagram of the OROMP algorithm is shown in Fig. 10.

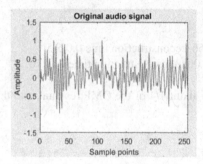

Fig. 6. Original audio signal diagram

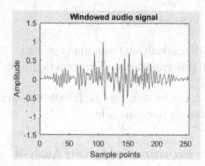

Fig. 7. Original audio signal diagram

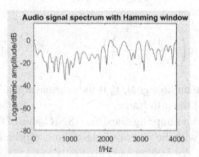

Fig. 8. Audio signal spectrum with Hamming window

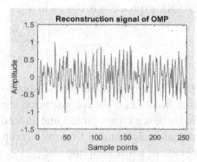

Fig. 9. OMP reconstruction signal diagram

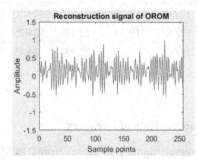

Fig. 10. OROMP reconstructed signal diagram

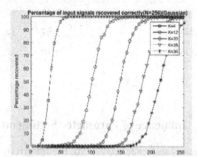

Fig. 11. Relation curve between signal sparsity K and probability of success in reconstruction

Result analysis:

OMP residual: ans1 = norm (x_r − x) = 0.0166, reconstruction time 0.0245;
OROMP residual: ans2 = norm (x_r − x) = 0.0043, reconstruction time 0.0216.

It can be seen that the OROMP residual is about 1/4 of the OMP residual, and the reconstruction time is less.

4.2 Reconstruction Quality Analysis

The audio signal is characterized by short-term stability, so the SNR must be measured every 20 ms and averaged over a long audio interval, which reflects the quantized quality of the input segments at different levels and has better characteristics than the subjective values. Therefore, the average signal-to-noise ratio (ASNR) is used to objectively test the quality of audio signal reconstruction and analyze the quality of signal reconstruction. The ASNR expression is shown in (6).

$$ASNR = \frac{1}{N} \sum_{n=1}^{N} \left(10 \lg \left(\frac{\|x_n\|_2^2}{\|x_n - \bar{x}_n\|_2^2} \right) \right) \tag{6}$$

Here, N is the total number of frames of the audio signal, x_n is the original signal of the n-th frame, $\bar{x}_n$ is the reconstructed signal of the n-th frame.

It can be seen from Table 1 that under different sampling rates, the ASNR value of the optimization algorithm is improved compared with the other two algorithms, especially in the case of a low sampling rate.

Table 1. Comparison of ASNR values of CS simulation results (dB)

Reconstruction algorithm	Sampling rate					
	0.1	0.2	0.3	0.4	0.5	0.6
OMP	7.42	14.09	17.50	19.56	21.39	23.10
ROMP	7.87	14.49	17.79	19.74	22.13	24.75
OROMP	10.40	16.57	18.04	20.05	22.78	24.45

4.3 Influence of Parameter Setting on the Success Rate of Recovery

When K is 4, 12, 20, 28, 36, the length of the observed signal Y increases from 0 to 250 with an interval of 10 points. The number of experiments repeated for each observed signal length was 50. The successful recovery criterion is the recovery residual less than 3.5.

Result analysis: The influence of signal length M and sparsity K on the percentage of correctly recovered input signals is shown in Fig. 11. The more data collected, the higher the probability of success, the smaller the sparsity K, and the fewer data needed to be collected.

In addition, the system carries out the online test for one month under the condition of mounting 10 terminals, simulating 200 terminals and maximum shunting 30. The delay of acquisition and broadcasting is stable between 100–200 ms, which shows that it has good stability.

5 Conclusions

In the paper, aiming at the problems of speech processing in campus broadcast system, in order to reduce the delay of speech acquisition, according to the principle that ROMP algorithm chooses a locally optimal solution to gradually approach the original signal through greedy thought every iteration, the inner product method of calculating the sensor matrix and margin is proposed only in the first iteration, and the subsequent iteration is replaced by vector subtraction. By using this method, the ability of fast reconstruction of the audio signal is obtained, and the ability and quality of fast propagation of multi-channel speech in the system are guaranteed.

Acknowledgments. This work was supported by the National Natural Science Foundation of China (61972147), the Natural Science Foundation of Hunan Province (2018JJ2606), the Major Industry Project of Hunan Manufacturing Strong Province (2017209, 2020NK2010), and the Innovation Training Program for College Students in 2020 of Hunan Province (S202010537039, SZ20200473, S202110537012X).

References

1. Candes, E.J., Tao, T.: Decoding by linear programming. IEEE Trans. Inf. Theory **51**(12), 4203–4215 (2005)
2. Baraniuk, R.G.: Compressive sensing. IEEE Signal Process. Mag. **24**(4), 118–121 (2007)
3. Do, T.T., Gan, L., Nguyen, N., et al.: Sparsity adaptive matching pursuit algorithm for practical compressed sensing. In: Conference on Signals, Systems & Computers, pp. 310–316. IEEE (2010)
4. Chang-Qing, Z., Yan-Pu, C.: Discrete cosine wavelet packet transform and speech signal compressed sensing. Acoustic Technol. **33**(01), 35–40 (2014)
5. Zhen-Zhen, Y., Zhen, Y., Lin-Hui, S.: Overview of orthogonal matching pursuit algorithms for signal compression and reconstruction. Signal Process. **29**(04), 486–496 (2013)
6. Jiang, X.: Audio signal sampling and reconstruction method based on perceptual compression theory, pp. 1–54. Master's thesis of Shanghai Jiao Tong University, Shanghai (2017)
7. Wang, W.-J.: Analysis and Research on speech characteristics based on compressed sensing theory, pp. 1–70. Master's thesis of Nanjing University of Posts and Telecommunications, Nanjing (2013)
8. Zhang, D.-F.: Research on robust speech compressed sensing reconstruction technology, pp. 1–54. Master's thesis of Nanjing University of Posts and Telecommunications, Nanjing (2017)
9. Wang, Y.-M.: Research and implementation of low rate speech coder based on compressed sensing, pp. 1–50. Master's thesis of Chongqing University of Posts and Telecommunications, Chongqing (2019)

10. Candes, E.: Signal recovery from random projections. Proc. SPIE **5674**(1), 76–86 (2005)
11. Gao, Y., Zang, M., Guo, F.: Research on speech compression based on wavelet transform and compressed sensing. Appl. Res. Comput. **34**(12), 3672–3674 (2017)
12. Derouaz, W., Meksen, T.: Compressed sensing-based speech compression using dictionary learning and IRLS algorithm. In: 2018 International Conference on Electrical Sciences and Technologies in Maghreb (CISTEM), Algiers, pp. 1–5 (2018)
13. Sahu, S., Rayavarapu, N.: Performance comparison of sparsifying basis functions for compressive speech enhancement. Int. J. Speech Technol. **22**, 769–783 (2019)
14. Gaurav Kumar, K., Chatterjee, B., Sen, S.: A 16 pJ/bit 0.1–15 Mbps compressive sensing IC with on-chip DWT sparsifier for audio signals. In: 2021 IEEE Custom Integrated Circuits Conference (CICC), pp. 1–2 (2021)
15. Baraniuk, R.G.: Compressed sensing. IEEE Signal Process. Mag. **24**(4), 118–121 (2007)
16. Wan, D.: Speech Compression Transmission and Reconstruction Based on Feature Information Assisted, pp. 1–56. Xihua University, Chengdu (2020)

Committee Selection Based on Game Theory in Sharding Blockchain

Jingrou Wu[ID] and Jin Zhang[✉][ID]

Southern University of Science and Technology, Shenzhen 518055, China
11960005@mail.sustech.edu.cn, zhangj4@sustech.edu.cn

Abstract. Blockchain has attracted the public's attention in recent years as a decentralized system. But it suffers from low transaction throughput and poor scalability. Sharding technology is proposed to improve blockchain's efficiency and performance using parallel processing. The key idea is to divide the miners into different shards or committees to process disjoint transaction sets. There are two kinds of committees in the sharding blockchain which bring miners different costs and rewards. One is dedicated to membership management and cross-shard transaction routing while the other is responsible for transaction validation. Miners have to decide which committee to participate in before they start working. In this paper, we study the problem of how much computational power would miners contribute to different kinds of committees in the view of game theory. We model the game as a two-stage hierarchical game and obtain the Nash equilibrium of this game. The experimental results show that both computational power limitation and system's parameters have effects on the final equilibrium.

Keywords: Proof of work · Sharding blockchain · Game theory

1 Introduction

The past decade has witnessed the rapid development of the blockchain since Satoshi Nakamoto proposed *Bitcoin* cryptocurrency in 2008 [17]. A blockchain is a transparent and traceable decentralized database with most miners' consensus. In a permissionless blockchain such as Bitcoin and Ethereum [23], proof of work (PoW) is the most common consensus protocol which requires computational power to solve PoW hash puzzles. High cost of PoW puzzles prevents malicious miners from attacking the blockchain system but it also leads to low transaction throughput and poor scalability.

To solve the efficiency problem, researches are conducted in scalability and throughput improvement, among which *sharding protocol* is a more general solution in blockchains' performance enhancement. Sharded blockchains allow miners to process diverse sets of transactions at the same time. Miners are divided into several shards or committees in which miners gather and process different sets of transactions in different shards. The shard size is unalterable because a larger

© ICST Institute for Computer Sciences, Social Informatics and Telecommunications Engineering 2022
Published by Springer Nature Switzerland AG 2022. All Rights Reserved
K. Wu et al. (Eds.): ICECI 2021, LNICST 437, pp. 13–28, 2022.
https://doi.org/10.1007/978-3-031-04231-7_2

shard size lowers the efficiency while a smaller shard size heightens the risk. The number of shards also keeps fixed as the network size is stable.

Miners' identities and group information need recording in the sharded blockchain system. In a permissioned system such as RSCoin [7], a trusted third-party, i.e., the central bank, is responsible for record and registration. While in a permissionless system without any trusted third-party such as RapidChain [25], a special committee, *Directory Service (DS) committee* or *Reference committee*, is required instead. Miners firstly compete for joining the DS committee. Then the rest miners compete for other shards' members. Since different kinds of committees bring different rewards and costs, it becomes a question for miners to decide which kind of committee to participate in and how much computational power to put in.

In non-sharding blockchain systems, especially Bitcoin, there are many studies to analyze miners' optimal actions. Most works [3,8,22] focus on participation of miners. That is, whether they join or leave in a non-sharding PoW blockchain. The computational power allocation is another field where miners decide how much computational power for investment [5,9]. However, these game models are not suitable in sharded blockchains because of different decision spaces and reward protocols. In the work [16], it analyzes actions of miners in a sharded blockchain with only non-DS committees hence they have no committee selection problem.

In this paper, we investigate the problem of miners decisions on different kinds of committees. We model the process as a two-stage hierarchical non-cooperative game. In the first stage, miners compete for the seat of the DS committee and then those who are not DS committees members play games during shards formation in order to maximize their utilities. The main contributions are as follows.

- We model the committee selection problem as a two-stage hierarchical game among miners.
- We prove the existence of Nash equilibrium of both sub-games. Further, we prove the uniqueness of Nash equilibrium of the DS committee member selection sub-game, i.e., the stage 1 sub-game.
- We conduct simulations to find that the game converges to the Nash equilibrium in practice and the experimental results show that computational power limitations affect miners' final decisions.

The rest of the paper is organized as follows. Section 2 describes the details of sharding protocols and Sect. 3 formulates the two-stage game model followed by Sect. 4 which gives an analysis of the Nash equilibrium in both sub-games. The experimental results are shown in Sect. 5 and related work are included in Sect. 6. We present the conclusion of the paper in Sect. 7.

2 Sharding Fundamentals

In this section, we firstly present the concept of sharded blockchain in detail and then describe the process of a blockchain with shards.

To support higher scalability and efficiency, the sharded blockchain partitions miners into different groups called shards or committees. Every shard can be regarded as a sub-network of the blockchain. Miners in the same shard process the same set of transactions by running Byzantine Fault-Tolerant (BFT) protocols (e.g. PBFT [4]) rather than PoW consensus protocols due to the small size of the shard. Therefore, the sharded blockchain is able to deal with different sets of transactions in parallel. The miners are chosen by PoW hash puzzles to join in these shards, which prevents Sybil Attack and guarantees miners' abilities to an extent. Given a sharded blockchain with a stable number of miners, the size of the shard and the number of shards remains fixed to keep a balance between efficiency and security. If there are more miners than required, some of them are not able to become shard members.

Meanwhile, a special committee, DS committee or reference committee, is required in the system for shards information record and miners registration. It is also responsible for cross-shard transactions which are transactions related to more than one shard. The DS committee provides routing services for such transactions. Besides, it aggregates micro blocks produced by other shards into the final block in the blockchain. Based on these functions, the DS committee members must be selected at first before other shards members. There are several diverse *DS committee member election* methods, among which the PoW puzzle is a common choice such as in Zilliqa [1]. To maintain the fixed size of the DS committee, the first-in-first-out policy is applied. The earliest committee member quits the DS committee and then the miner who solves the PoW puzzle at first becomes the new member. Overall, the DS committee and other shards have different duties in the sharded blockchain system and have different PoW puzzles to solve during selection.

For the sake of fairness, all committees shuffle after a period of time called *epoch* in order to prevent collusion. At the beginning of the epoch, the DS committee is formed firstly and then other shards are shaped. After committee formations, miners process transactions in parallel, generating m micro blocks for each shard during the epoch. At the end of the epoch, the system distributes rewards to miners and miners prepare themselves for the next epoch.

3   Committee Selection Game

In this section, we formulate the committee selection game as a two-stage hierarchical game. We assume all miners are honest but selfish and miners do not collude with each other. To maximize their own utilities, miners decided the amount of computational power to contribute to different committee formation processes.

3.1   Problem Formulation

We consider the situation where miners are able to make decisions to contribute how much computational power to the first PoW hash puzzle PoW_1 and the second puzzle PoW_2 on themselves. They are selfish and therefore they only care about their own profits while doing choices. We formulate the Computational Power Game $\mathbb{G}$ as a non-cooperative game denoted by $\mathbb{G} = (\mathcal{P}, \mathcal{S}, \mathcal{U})$, where $\mathcal{P}$ is a set of players, $\mathcal{S}$ is the players' strategy space and $\mathcal{U}$ is the players' utility values.

Players ($\mathcal{P}$). Players are miners who are willing to participate in the game including *DS Committee Member Selection* as well as *Shards Formation*, at a given epoch. The DS committee with the size of n_1 requires 1 new member and other shards need n_2 miners at a time. Let's assume all players are shortsighted which means they only aim at the current game without considering the following repeated game processes. At a one-shot game, they make decisions merely dependent on the final utility.

With N players of computational power limitations $\bar{\mathbf{X}} = \{\bar{x}_1, \bar{x}_2, \cdots, \bar{x}_N\}$ in a game, players firstly play the DS Committee Member Selection sub-game where only one player is able to become the new committee member. Then the rest $N - 1$ players compete for n_2 seats in shards.

Strategies ($\mathcal{S}$). For each sub-game, the strategies of players are to decide the amount of computational power x_i to put in. If the computational power $x_i = 0$, it means that the player does not participate in the process.

In the stage 1 sub-game, miners contribute computational power to solve the PoW_1 puzzle. Once the ith miner has been chosen as a new member, he would sign $m+m_e$ signatures where m is the number of other shard members' signatures and m_e is the number of extra signatures as a DS committee member. Given the total system reward R, a part of reward aR is distributed to $N_s = n_1 + n_2$ all committee members as fixed reward $r_f = \frac{aR}{N_s}$, while the rest reward $(1-a)R$ is assigned to members according to their workload, i.e., the number of signatures. Every valid signature is rewarded with $r_s = \frac{(1-a)R}{N_s m + n_1 m_e}$. Hence, the reward of a DS committee member is composed of two parts, the fixed reward r_f and the workload reward $r_s(m + m_e)$:

$$r_1 = r_f + r_s(m + m_e) \tag{1}$$

Similarly, in the stage 2 sub-game, successful miners with m signatures gain r_2 with a fixed component r_f and a workload component $r_s m$ as follows:

$$r_2 = r_f + r_s m \tag{2}$$

Utilities ($\mathcal{U}$). Given the rewards mentioned above, we consider the expectation of rewards as profits for every miner.

$$r_{1,i} = p(x_i; \mathbf{X_{-i}}) r_1 \tag{3}$$

$$r_{2,i} = p(x_i; \mathbf{X_{-i}}) r_2 \tag{4}$$

where $p(x_i; \mathbf{X_{-i}})$ is the probability of the ith miner becoming a committee member.

The cost is composed of 4 aspects: (1) the boot loss cost for PoW puzzle solving, (2) the energy cost, (3) the cost for signatures and (4) the cost for fixed assets depreciation, which is denoted by:

$$c(x_i, m_i) = c_f x_i + c_e t x_i + c_s m_i + c_r \frac{x_i}{\bar{x}_i} \tag{5}$$

where $c_f x_i$ is the boot loss cost for using x_i computational power, $c_e t x_i$ is the energy cost with t the time for solving the PoW puzzle, $c_s m_i$ is the workload cost and $c_r \frac{x_i}{\bar{x}_i}$ is the fixed assets depreciation cost.

We assume that are enough miners in every epoch to form committees. In this way, the miner's utility is equal to the expectation of the rewards minus the cost:

$$U(x_i; \mathbf{X}_{-i}) = p(x_i; \mathbf{X}_{-i})r - c(x_i, m_i) \tag{6}$$

where $\mathbf{X}_{-\mathbf{i}} = \{x_1, x_2, \ldots\}$ is a vector of other miners' strategies, r is the general symbol of reward and m_i is the number of signatures the ith miner will sign. The details of utility are analyzed in Sect. 3.2.

3.2   Hierarchical Game Model

Because the DS committee member selection and shards formation are two different processes, we model the game $\mathcal{G}$ as a two-stage game, the stage 1 DS committee member selection game (CSG) and the stage 2 shards formation game (SFG) $\mathcal{G}_2$. All miners firstly participate in $\mathcal{G}_1$ and then miners who fail to become a DS committee member compete for $\mathcal{G}_2$.

DS Committee Member Selection Sub-game. In this sub-game, only one player is able to get into the new DS committee which is similar to Bitcoin where only one block is generated in a period of time. We consider the PoW puzzles solving as a random process in which miners have to try a certain of times to find the final solution. It is formulated as *Poisson process* in former works [19,21,22]. We assume that unit computational power is able to find s possible answers per unit time and it requires k_1 attempts on average to solve the PoW_1 puzzle. We define the difficulty factor as $d_1 = \frac{k_1}{s}$ and hence the time required for finding one puzzle solution is drawn from the exponential distribution with a parameter $\theta = \frac{d_1}{x_i + Y}$ where $Y = \sum_{i \neq j} x_j$ is the total computation power in the system except for x_i. That is, the expectation of the time for the first solution found is θ. It is also the time t required for any players in this sub-game because whenever a solution is found, all other miners stop solving. As for the probability, it is only related to the computational power due to the memoryless property of the exponential distribution. It is represented as $p(x_i; \mathbf{X}_{-i}) = \frac{x_i}{x_i + \sum_{j \neq i} x_j}$. Therefore, the utility for players in this sub-game is the reward minus cost:

$$U_1(x_i; \mathbf{X}_{-i}) = \frac{x_i}{x_i + \sum_{j \neq i} x_j} r_1 - c(x_i, m + m_e) \tag{7}$$

where r_1 is the reward of the DS committee member and $c(x_i, m+m_e) = c_f x_i + c_e d_1 \frac{x_i}{x_i+Y} + c_s(m + m_e) + c_r \frac{x_i}{x_i}$ is the cost.

We define the best response problem of stage 1 sub-game as:

Definition 1. *The best response problem of the DS committee selection sub-game (PoW$_1$) can be formulated as:*

$$\max_{0 \leq x_i \leq \bar{x}_i} U_1(x_i; \mathbf{X_{-i}}) \tag{8}$$

which means to find the best strategy, i.e., the amount of computational power to maximize the miner's utility.

Shards Formation Sub-game. In this sub-game, n_2 out of $N-1$ players are chosen as shard members. Different from the DS committee selection sub-game in Sect. 3.2, time for solving PoW_2 puzzles is not able to be drawn from total computational power because once a player successfully finds the solution, the process becomes a different Poisson process. Since it is difficult to predict which player has been selected as a new member, it is unpractical to model the time t from the view of total computational power. We formulate the time t in the aspect of individual solving process. That is, for each player, the process of PoW puzzle solving is a Poisson process with the parameter $\theta = \frac{d_2}{x_i}$ where $d_2 = \frac{k_2}{s}$ is the PoW_2's difficulty coefficient and k_2 is the number of attempts to find a solution. We assume that the DS committee publishes shards information after the window size t_2 and hence for those who are not selected as new members, they keep looking for a solution for t_2 as well. The probability of success is a sum of possibilities where the miner is chosen at jth:

$$p_2(x_i; \mathbf{X_{-i}}) = \sum_{j=1}^{n_2} p_{2, \mathbf{X_j}}(x_i; \mathbf{X_{-i}}) \tag{9}$$

where $\mathbf{X_j}$ is the set of permutations of miners' computational power when the ith miner's decision x_i at the jth position.

The probability of a miner with x_i computational power chosen as the jth shard member is the sum of probability for every permutation in $\mathbf{X_j}$:

$$p_{2, \mathbf{X_j}}(x_i; \mathbf{X_{-i}}) = \sum_{\mathbf{x_j} \in \mathbf{X_j}} \prod_{k=1}^{n_2} \frac{x_{j_k}}{Y + x_i - \sum_{l=1}^{k-1} x_{j_l}} \tag{10}$$

where $\mathbf{x_j}$ is the element (permutation) of the set $\mathbf{X_j}$ and x_{j_k} means the computational power of the kth miner in the permutation $\mathbf{x_j}$.

For example, if there are 3 players compete for 2 seats, the probability $p_2(x_i; X_{-i}) = \frac{x_i}{Y+x_i} + \sum_{j \in N} \frac{x_j}{Y+x_i} \cdot \frac{x_i}{Y+x_i-x_j}$ after simplifications is the sum of the possibility for the first competition and the possibility for the second competition. Hence the utility for players in this sub-game is composed of the two parts: (1) When the miner succeeds, the utility is the rewards minus the cost with $\frac{d_2}{x_i}$ time and (2) When the miner fails, the utility is the cost only with t_2 time. Since the miner has the probability of p_2 for success, the utility is simplified as:

$$U_2(x_i; \mathbf{X_{-i}}) = p_2(x_i; \mathbf{X_{-i}})R_2 - Cx_i \qquad (11)$$

where $R_2 = r_2 + c_e t_2 x_i - c_e d_2 - c_s m$ and $C = c_e t_2 + c_f + \frac{c_r}{\bar{x}}$.

Similarly, we define the best response of stage 2 sub-game as:

Definition 2. *The best response of shards formation sub-game PoW_2 can be formulated as:*

$$\max_{0 \le x_i \le \bar{x}_i} U_2(x_i; \mathbf{X_{-i}})$$

$$\text{s.t. } x_{PoW_1} \notin \mathbf{X_{-i}} \qquad (12)$$

where x_{PoW_1} is the computational power of the miner who has become a DS committee member.

4   Game Analysis

In this section, we provide the analysis of the two-stage game $\mathcal{G}$. We show that it exists a unique Nash equilibrium [18] in this game $\mathcal{G}$, which defines the optimal strategy for miners in both stages.

We firstly prove the existence of Nash equilibrium in stage 1 sub-game which is further proved to be unique. Then, we give a solution of shards formation sub-game based on the stage 1's result. In the next round $t+1$, validators change their strategies according to the difference between the utility of online and the utility of offline given their own network conditions and the current states $D_i(\theta_i, A_{t+1})$ where A_{t+1} is all players' decisions at the round $t + 1$.

4.1   DS Committee Member Selection Sub-game

We analyze players' decisions in DS committee selection game here. According to (8), the utility of a player does not only subject to his own computational power contributed but also depends on others' behaviours. Given others' choices $\mathbf{X_{-i}} = \{x_1, x_2, \dots\}$, the *ith* miner chooses the proper computational power x_i to maximize his utility, namely, $x_i = \arg\max_{0 \le x_i \le \bar{x}_i} U_1(x_i; \mathbf{X_{-i}})$. In a non-cooperative game, the *ith* miner uses this x_i as his best response which is stated in the following theorem.

Theorem 1 (Best response). *Given $\mathbf{X_{-i}}$, the best response of ith miner in DS committee member selection sub-game is*

$$x_i^* = \begin{cases} \sqrt{\dfrac{AY}{c_i}} - Y, & otherwise & (13a) \\\\ 0, & \sqrt{\dfrac{AY}{c_i}} < Y & (13b) \end{cases}$$

where $A = r_1 - c_e d_1$ and $c_i = c_f + \frac{c_r}{\bar{x}_i}$

Proof. We use $U_{1,i}$ to denote the the utility of the *ith* miner in the DS committee member selection sub-game. The first and second derivatives of $U_{1,i}$ respect to x_i are:

$$\frac{\partial U_{1,i}}{\partial x_i} = \frac{AY}{(x_i+Y)^2} - c_i \tag{14}$$

$$\frac{\partial^2 U_{1,i}}{\partial x_i^2} = -\frac{2AY}{(X+Y)^3} \tag{15}$$

The second derivative of $U_{1,i}$ with respect to x_i is always negative so that $U_{1,i}$ is a concave function in x_i. Let the first derivative of $U_{1,i}$ with respect to x_i become zero. Then, $x_i = \sqrt{\frac{AY}{c_i}} - Y$. If $\sqrt{\frac{AY}{c_i}} - Y < 0$, it means that no matter how much computational power the player contribute, it always brings negative utility. Therefore, the player will not participate in the stage 1 sub-game and hence $x_i = 0$.

Now we consider the situation under the Nash equilibrium in which every player has his own best response $x_i^*, i \in N$ and none of them will alter the strategy because they will not get more rewards in such case. We prove that such Nash equilibrium is unique.

Theorem 2 (Uniqueness of Nash equilibrium). *There exists a unique Nash equilibrium in DS committee member selection sub-game and the optimal computation power for each player is given by* (13a) *and* (13b).

Proof. It is proven in [24] that if the best function is positive, monotonic and scalable, the game has a unique Nash equilibrium. So we prove these properties of the best function as follows.

Under the Nash equilibrium, every player makes his best response with respect to others' strategies. So, the computational power should be:

$$x_i^* = \sqrt{\frac{AY^*}{c_i}} - Y^* \tag{16}$$

where $Y^* = \sum_{i \neq j} x_j^*$.

We add Y^* on both side and the square of it is $(x_i^* + Y^*)^2 = \frac{AY}{c_i}$ so we have

$$x_i^* = CP^* - \frac{CP^{*2}c_i}{A} \tag{17}$$

where $CP^* = \sum_{i \in \mathbf{X}} x_i^*$. Sum up all the N equations of each player, we get

$$CP^* = \frac{(N-1)A}{\sum_{i \in N} c_i} \tag{18}$$

Replace CP^* with (18), we can get

$$x_i^* = \frac{(N-1)A}{\sum_{i \in N} c_i} - \frac{(\frac{(N-1)A}{\sum_{i \in N} c_i})^2 c_i}{A} \tag{19}$$

It is easy to prove this is a positive, monotonic and scalable function. Hence, the sub-game has unique Nash equilibrium.

4.2   Shards Formation Sub-game

Since players in this stage have already known about who has been chosen as a new DS committee, they only play game with the rest $N-1$ players. Similarly, the miners' strategies are the set of computational powers $\mathbf{X} = \{x_i | 0 \le x_i \le \bar{x}_i\}$ and utility functions are analyzed above.

Theorem 3 (Existence of Nash equilibrium). *There exists at least one Nash equilibrium in shards formation sub-game (choosing n_2 from $N-1$ miners) when $\bar{Y} < \frac{(n_2+1)B}{2c_e t_2}$, where $B = r_2 - c_e d_2 - c_s m$, $\bar{Y} = \sum_{j \ne i} \bar{x}_j$ and $n_2 \ge 2$.*

Proof. According to [12], when the strategy set is compact and convex and the utility function is a continuous function in the profile of strategies $\mathbf{s} \in \mathcal{S}$ and quasi-concave in s_i for every player, the game has at least one pure-strategy Nash equilibrium. Since the strategy set is compact and convex and the utility function is continuous obviously, we only need to prove its quasi-concave.

Because concave functions are always quasi-concave, we prove the concavity of the utility function in the following.

Lemma 1 (Concave utility function). *The utility function $U_2(x_i; \mathbf{X}_{-i})$ of miners in $\mathcal{G}_2$ is concave when $\forall n_2 \ge 2, \bar{Y} < \frac{(n_2+1)B}{2c_e t_2}$.*

Proof. We present the utility function $U_2(x_i; \mathbf{X}_{-i})$ and the probability function $p_2(x_i; \mathbf{X}_{-i})$ of the ith miner as $U_{2,i}$ and $p_{2,i}$ respectively. The first derivative of the utility function is

$$\frac{\partial U_{2,i}}{\partial x_i} = \frac{\partial p_{2,i}}{\partial x_i} R_{2,i} + p_{2,i} \frac{\partial R_{2,i}}{\partial x_i} - C \tag{20}$$

and the second derivative is

$$\frac{\partial^2 U_{2,i}}{\partial x_i^2} = \frac{\partial^2 p_{2,i}}{\partial x_i^2} R_{2,i}$$
$$+ 2 \frac{\partial p_{2,i}}{\partial x_i} \frac{\partial R_{2,i}}{\partial x_i} \tag{21}$$
$$+ \frac{\partial^2 R_{2,i}}{\partial x_i^2} p_{2,i}$$

where $U_{2,i}$ and $p_{2,i}$ are the utility and probability function of the ith miner in stage 2 sub-game.

Because $R_{2,i}$ is the linear function and hence $\frac{\partial^2 R_{2,i}}{\partial x_i^2} = 0$. Therefore, we have $\frac{\partial^2 R_{2,i}}{\partial x_i^2} p_{2,i} = 0$. We only need to prove $\frac{\partial^2 p_{2,i}}{\partial x_i^2} R_{2,i} + 2 \frac{\partial p_{2,i}}{\partial x_i} \frac{\partial R_{2,i}}{\partial x_i} < 0$ subject to $\bar{Y} < \frac{n_2(N-1)B}{2(N-n_2)C_e t_2}$.

After simplification, the first derivative of the probability function $p_{2,i}$ of the ith miner is:

$$\frac{\partial p_{2,i}}{\partial x_i} = \sum_{\mathbf{x_j} \in \mathbf{X_j}} \sum_{k=1}^{j-1} \frac{\prod_{l=1}^{j-1} x_{j_l}}{\prod_{s=0}^{j-2} (Y + x_i - \sum_{l=1}^{s} x_{j_l})^{a_k(s)}} \tag{22}$$

where $j = n_2 + 1$ and $a_k(s)$ is:

$$a_k(s) = \begin{cases} 2, & s = k, \\ 1, & s \neq k. \end{cases} \tag{23}$$

The second derivative has similar structure, summing up all second derivative of items listed above. We present the second derivative of the kth single item $T_k = \frac{\prod_{l=1}^{j-1} x_{jk}}{\prod_{s=0}^{j-2}(Y + x_i - \sum_{l=1}^{s} x_{jl})^{a_k(s)}}$ for example.

$$\frac{\partial T_k}{\partial x_i} = \sum_{s=0}^{j-2} \frac{-(a_k(s)+1)}{(Y + x_i - \sum_{l=1}^{s} x_{jl})} T_k \tag{24}$$

If we prove that $F_k = \frac{\partial T_k}{\partial x_i} R_{2,i} + 2T_k c_e t_2 < 0$ for every single item in the first derivative of $p_{2,i}$, then we have $\frac{\partial^2 p_{2,i}}{\partial x_i^2} R_{2,i} + 2\frac{\partial p_{2,i}}{\partial x_i} \frac{\partial R_{2,i}}{\partial x_i} < 0$.

We can transform the F_k as:

$$\begin{aligned} F_k &= c_e t_2 \left(\frac{\partial T_k}{\partial x_i} \left(\frac{B}{c_e t_2} + x_i \right) + 2T_k \right) \\ &= T_k c_e t_2 \left(\sum_{s=0}^{j-2} \left(D_s \left(\frac{B}{c_e t_2} + x_i \right) + \frac{2}{n_2} \right) \right) \end{aligned} \tag{25}$$

where $D_s = \frac{-(a_k(s)+1)}{(Y + x_i - \sum_{l=1}^{s} x_{jl})}$.

We only need to prove $Q(x_i) = \sum_{s=0}^{j-2} D_s(\frac{B}{c_e t_2} + x_i) + \frac{2}{n_2}$ is less than 0 because $T_k c_e t_2$ is always positive. Since it is a monotonically decrease function respect to x_i, we just need prove $Q(0) < 0$ when $x_i = 0$.

$$\begin{aligned} Q(0) &= \sum_{s=0}^{j-2} \frac{-(a_k(s)+1)}{(Y - \sum_{l=1}^{s} x_{jl})} \frac{B}{c_e t_2} + \frac{2}{n_2} \\ &< \sum_{s=0}^{j-2} \frac{-(a_k(s)+1)}{Y} \frac{B}{c_e t_2} + \frac{2}{n_2} \\ &= \frac{-(n_2+1)}{Y} \frac{B}{c_e t_2} + 2 \\ &< \frac{-(n_2+1)}{\bar{Y}} \frac{B}{c_e t_2} + 2 \end{aligned} \tag{26}$$

Let $\frac{-(n_2+1)}{\bar{Y}} \frac{B}{c_e t_2} + 2 < 0$, we have $\bar{Y} < \frac{n_2+1}{2} \frac{B}{c_e t_2}$ which is consistent with the condition.

Hence, $U_2(x_i; \mathbf{X_{-i}})$ is concave when $\bar{Y} < \frac{(n_2+1)B}{2c_e t_2}$.

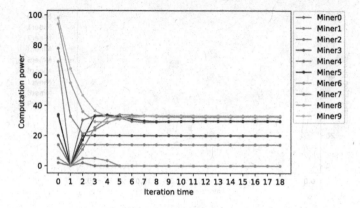

Fig. 1. Iterations in CSG.

5 Experimental Results

In this section, we conduct numerical simulations to find the Nash equilibrium in practical and evaluate different parameters' effects on players' strategies and utilities.

5.1 Game Analysis

The setting of our simulations are as follows. It has total $N = 10$ miners and $n_2 = 2$ required in other shards. The total reward is $R = 500$ and the reward ratio is $a = 0.75$. There are $m = 100$ blocks in an epoch. The cost coefficients are as follows: the electricity cost $c_e = 1$, the boot loss cost and the fixed assets depreciation cost $c_f = c_r = 0.5$ and the cost of each signature is ignored, that is, $c_s = 0$. The difficulty degrees are $d_1 = 2$ and $d_2 = 1$. The window size of the stage 2 process is $t_2 = 2$. In the one-short game, miners originally contribute the maximum computational power and their computational power limits are $\bar{\mathbf{X}} = \{2, 5, 14, 20, 33, 34, 69, 78, 94, 98\}$. As Fig. 1 and Fig. 2 shows, most players after several iterations converge to their final strategies where the $5th$ miner (Miner4) is chosen as the new DS committee member. Players with higher computational power are more likely to contribute more as well.

Figure 3 shows the final computational power miners contribute and the expectation of utilities they gain in both stages where the $5th$ miner (Miner4) is starred as a new DS committee member. Miners with less computational power are not willing to participate in the selection game while those who have more computational power are not likely to put all into the game. Compared the stage 1 with the stage 2, we found that players with high computational power would like to contribute more to stage 2 than stage 1 because they are more likely to be chosen in stage 2 than stage 1.

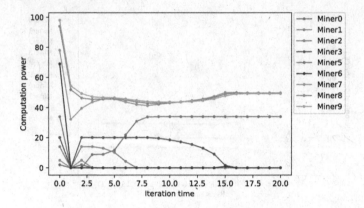

Fig. 2. Iterations in SFG.

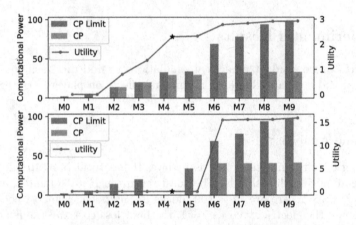

Fig. 3. Computational power and utility

5.2 Cost Coefficients Analysis

In this subsection, we draw attention to the impact of system parameters, especially the cost coefficients. All analyses are based on the stage 1 sub-game since stage 2 sub-game has a similar tendency.

In the setting as mentioned above, it presents that with the increase of the electricity cost c_e, miners are less likely to contribute computational power to the game. However, they receive more rewards because the computational powers of others decrease and therefore they have higher probabilities of success. In Fig. 4, we show some typical miners' computation powers and utilities where a miner gives up the game, a miner always put all computational power into the game and two other miners adjust their computational powers according to different electricity cost.

Different from the effect of electricity cost, the impacts of the boot loss c_f are more complex. When c_f is small, every player is willing to contribute all their

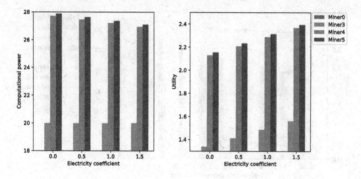

Fig. 4. Computational power and utility with different c_e

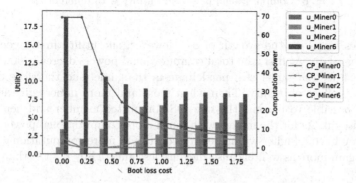

Fig. 5. Computational power and utility with different c_f

computational powers because it costs little to turn on rigs. However, when the cost gets larger, miners with few computation powers quit the game because the cost and others' computational powers are larger, while those who have medium computation powers still contribute all powers. But, players with higher power limitations decrease the powers due to the increment of boot loss cost as the lines in Fig. 5 show. When the costs keep increasing, players with more computational powers cut down the contributions because it cost more, while miners with fewer computational powers are likely to put more because the total computational powers are less than before and hence they have higher probabilities to gain rewards. As for the utility, miners with less computational powers gain more rewards while miners with more computational powers gain fewer rewards with the increase of boot loss cost.

As for the fixed assets depreciation cost c_r, there are three different situations as Fig. 6 shows. Miners with few computational powers as the $1st$ miner and the $2nd$ miner decrease their contributions when c_r exceeds a certain value because the cost has the most impact on these miners. Meanwhile, their utilities go down not only because the cost increases but also because players with higher limitations are likely to put more computational powers reducing their competitiveness. Miners with medium computational powers as the $4th$ miner

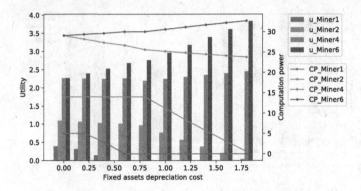

Fig. 6. Computational power and utility with different c_r

contributes less with the growth of c_r. However, the utility firstly goes down and then goes up. At first, the total computational powers decrease slowly since miners such as $2nd$ miner still participate in the game, and therefore the cost is the main effect on utility. Then when more and more miners give up, they are more possible to become the new DS committee member and hence their utilities rise up. As for the miners with much more computational powers as $6th$ miner, they have a higher willingness to contribute more computational powers and they gain more as well because they are less affected by high c_r than others.

6   Related Work

Sharding protocols are used in distributed databases [6, 11] to achieve higher performance in which nodes are reliable at first. Then George Danezis and Sarah Meiklejohn [7] applied such ideas to a permissioned blockchain system which provides strong transparency and auditability guarantees for the central bank. Then, *ELASTICO* [15] was proposed later for a permissionless blockchain where miners are not trusted. However, the sharded permissionless blockchain framework in *ELASTICO* lacks details of rules for partitions and it only supports network sharding and transaction sharding ignoring stage sharding. OmniLedger [13] and RapidChain [25] supports stage sharding which allows miners to keep the part of the blockchain instead of the whole chain to save individual storage room. OmniLedge [13] also came up with an identity blockchain to record committees information while RapidChain [25] recommended reference committee instead.

Game theory has been widely used in blockchain systems especially the analysis of incentive and security. Some work [3, 22] formulates the individual mining process in Bitcoin facing different rewards mechanisms, while some [14] study miners' investment strategies in mining pools. As for the security, most work focus on *selfish mining* where miners might break the rule to maximize their utilities. For example, Y. Zhen et al. [26] consider the situation when miners do not publish the block as soon as possible but hold them for higher utilities. Fork chain selections are studied in [3,10,14]. However, all these work only consider the blockchain without shard which is not able to apply to sharded blockchains directly.

There is few work about game models in blockchain with shards. The work [16] firstly analyzed miners' behaviours in a sharded blockchain and came up with incentive mechanisms to motivate miners to participate in the system. However, it only considers the sharded blockchain system with one-layer committees such as ELASTICO. A cooperative game is formulated in [2] to form shards, which is not suitable in a PoW competition blockchain system. Zhengwei Ni [20] et al. model the consensus provision at the node level for multiple blockchains with shard as an evolutionary game which focus on sharded blockchain applications rather than itself.

7   Conclusion

In this paper, we have investigated the committee selection in a permissionless sharded blockchain with two-layer committees. We model the system as a hierarchy two-stage game model including the DS committee selection sub-game and shards formation sub-game and prove the existence of Nash equilibrium in both sub-games and the uniqueness of the DS committee selection sub-game. Then, we evaluate the game under different system parameters and the experimental results have illustrated that miners with higher computational power limitations are likely to contribute more powers to the game. It also shows that miners with high computational powers are more resistant to fixed assets depreciation cost than others, but they are more sensitive to boot loss cost.

Acknowledgement. This work was supported in part by the National Natural Science Foundation of China under Grant No. 61701216, Shenzhen Science, Technology and Innovation Commission Basic Research Project under Grant No. JCYJ20180507181527806, Guangdong Provincial Key Laboratory (Grant No. 2020B121201001) and "Guangdong Innovative and Entrepreneurial Research Team Program" (2016ZT06G587) and the "Shenzhen Sci-Tech Fund" (KYTDPT20181011104007).

References

1. The Zilliqa Project (2017). https://zilliqa.com
2. Asheralieva, A., Niyato, D.: Reputation-based coalition formation for secure self-organized and scalable sharding in IoT blockchains with mobile-edge computing. IEEE Internet Things J. **7**(12), 11830–11850 (2020)
3. Carlsten, M., Kalodner, H., Weinberg, S.M., Narayanan, A.: On the instability of bitcoin without the block reward. In: Proceedings of the 2016 ACM SIGSAC Conference on Computer and Communications Security, pp. 154–167 (2016)
4. Castro, M., Liskov, B., et al.: Practical byzantine fault tolerance. In: OSDI 1999, pp. 173–186 (1999)
5. Chiu, J., Koeppl, T.: Incentive compatibility on the blockchain. In: Trockel, W. (ed.) Social Design. SED, pp. 323–335. Springer, Cham (2019). https://doi.org/10.1007/978-3-319-93809-7_20

6. Corbett, J.C., et al.: Spanner: Google's globally distributed database. ACM Trans. Comput. Syst. (TOCS) **31**(3), 1–22 (2013)
7. Danezis, G., Meiklejohn, S.: Centrally banked cryptocurrencies. arXiv preprint arXiv:1505.06895 (2015)
8. Dhamal, S., Chahed, T., Ben-Ameur, W., Altman, E., Sunny, A., Poojary, S.: A stochastic game framework for analyzing computational investment strategies in distributed computing with application to blockchain mining. arXiv preprint arXiv:1809.03143 (2018)
9. Dimitri, N.: Bitcoin mining as a contest. Ledger **2**, 31–37 (2017)
10. Eyal, I.: The miner's dilemma. In: 2015 IEEE Symposium on Security and Privacy, pp. 89–103. IEEE (2015)
11. Glendenning, L., Beschastnikh, I., Krishnamurthy, A., Anderson, T.: Scalable consistency in scatter. In: Proceedings of the Twenty-Third ACM Symposium on Operating Systems Principles, pp. 15–28 (2011)
12. Han, Z., Niyato, D., Saad, W., Baar, T., Hjrungnes, A.: Game Theory in Wireless and Communication Networks: Theory, Models, and Applications, 1st edn. Cambridge University Press, Cambridge (2012)
13. Kokoris-Kogias, E., Jovanovic, P., Gasser, L., Gailly, N., Syta, E., Ford, B.: OmniLedger: a secure, scale-out, decentralized ledger via sharding. In: 2018 IEEE Symposium on Security and Privacy (SP), pp. 583–598. IEEE (2018)
14. Kroll, J.A., Davey, I.C., Felten, E.W.: The economics of bitcoin mining, or bitcoin in the presence of adversaries. In: Proceedings of WEIS, vol. 2013, p. 11 (2013)
15. Luu, L., Narayanan, V., Zheng, C., Baweja, K., Gilbert, S., Saxena, P.: A secure sharding protocol for open blockchains. In: Proceedings of the 2016 ACM SIGSAC Conference on Computer and Communications Security, pp. 17–30 (2016)
16. Manshaei, M.H., Jadliwala, M., Maiti, A., Fooladgar, M.: A game-theoretic analysis of shard-based permissionless blockchains. IEEE Access **6**, 78100–78112 (2018)
17. Nakamoto, S.: A peer-to-peer electronic cash system (2008). https://bitcoin.org
18. Nash, J.: Non-cooperative games. Ann. Math. 286–295 (1951)
19. Nayak, K., Kumar, S., Miller, A., Shi, E.: Stubborn mining: generalizing selfish mining and combining with an eclipse attack. In: 2016 IEEE European Symposium on Security and Privacy (EuroS&P), pp. 305–320. IEEE (2016)
20. Ni, Z., Wang, W., Kim, D.I., Wang, P., Niyato, D.: Evolutionary game for consensus provision in permissionless blockchain networks with shards. In: ICC 2019–2019 IEEE International Conference on Communications (ICC), pp. 1–6. IEEE (2019)
21. Sapirshtein, A., Sompolinsky, Y., Zohar, A.: Optimal selfish mining strategies in bitcoin. In: Grossklags, J., Preneel, B. (eds.) FC 2016. LNCS, vol. 9603, pp. 515–532. Springer, Heidelberg (2017). https://doi.org/10.1007/978-3-662-54970-4_30
22. Tsabary, I., Eyal, I.: The gap game. In: Proceedings of the 2018 ACM SIGSAC conference on Computer and Communications Security, pp. 713–728 (2018)
23. Wood, G.: Ethereum: a secure decentralised generalised transaction ledger (2014). https://ethereum.org
24. Yates, R.D.: A framework for uplink power control in cellular radio systems. IEEE J. Sel. Areas Commun. **13**(7), 1341–1347 (1995)
25. Zamani, M., Movahedi, M., Raykova, M.: Rapidchain: scaling blockchain via full sharding. In: Proceedings of the 2018 ACM SIGSAC Conference on Computer and Communications Security, pp. 931–948 (2018)
26. Zhen, Y., Yue, M., Zhong-yu, C., Chang-bing, T., Xin, C.: Zero-determinant strategy for the algorithm optimize of blockchain pow consensus. In: 2017 36th Chinese Control Conference (CCC), pp. 1441–1446. IEEE (2017)

Green Transition Driven Carbon Trading Mechanism and Design Based on Urban Vehicle Trajectory Data

Wenjie Chen[1] , Xiaogang Wu[1]([✉]) , and Zhu Xiao[2]

[1] Business College, Central South University of Forestry and Technology, Changsha 410004, China
t20142193@csuft.edu.cn, Xiaogang121488@163.com
[2] College of Computer Science and Electronic Engineering, Hunan University, Changsha 410082, China
zhxiao@hnu.edu.cn

Abstract. As the fastest growing source of carbon emissions in the world, road traffic must carry out green transformation in order to achieve carbon neutrality, it is one of the feasible ways to establish private car carbon trading market and carry out personal carbon trade. Based on the big data of urban vehicle trajectory, this paper uses BP neural network to predict the carbon emissions of urban vehicles. Next, the total carbon emission cap is set by combining the predicted amount with the emission reduction, and the carbon consumers of private cars will be equally distributed free of charge based on the total emissions quota. In addition, this paper introduces block chain technology into the carbon trading system and designs a main-side block chain architecture to isolate the data business and financial business of carbon trade. Next, this paper establishes a transaction matching strategy to maximize the overall benefit. Finally, this paper verifies the proposed carbon-trading mechanism for private car through simulation design, and the results show that carbon-trading mechanism for private cars driven by green transition designed in this paper is feasible. It can play a certain role in emission reduction and market guidance.

Keywords: Green transition · Carbon trading · Carbon emission prediction · Carbon quota allocation

1 Introduction

Mitigation of climate warming has been a major problem for human beings. As early as 1992, the United Nations Conference on Environment and Development adopted the Framework and Convention on Climate Change to discuss climate issues in Rio. The Paris Agreement proposed to keep the temperature rise within 1.5 °C in 2015. At the United Nations General Assembly in 2020, China made it clear that it would strive to achieve a peak in carbon dioxide emissions by 2030 and achieve carbon neutrality by 2060 [1].

© ICST Institute for Computer Sciences, Social Informatics and Telecommunications Engineering 2022
Published by Springer Nature Switzerland AG 2022. All Rights Reserved
K. Wu et al. (Eds.): ICECI 2021, LNICST 437, pp. 29–45, 2022.
https://doi.org/10.1007/978-3-031-04231-7_3

The Energy Foundation released China's Carbon Neutral Comprehensive Report 2020 in December 2020, it pointed out that the carbon emission of China's transportation industry in 2050 should be reduced by 80% compared with that in 2015 [2]. According to the International Energy Agency in 2019, the transportation industry accounts for 24.6% of global carbon emissions and road traffic accounts for 73.8% of carbon dioxide emissions from transportation industry. As for China, China's carbon dioxide emissions were 10.2 billion tonnages; the transportation industry accounts for about 10%, and road traffic accounts for 84.1% of carbon dioxide emissions from the transportation industry [3]. Carbon emissions from road traffic have become the largest sector of the transportation industry, which is mainly due to the large increase in the number of cars in China. The rapid growth of private car ownership poses a huge challenge for China to achieve carbon peak by 2030, how to reduce carbon dioxide emission of private cars in China, it is of great significance to study the feasible carbon emission trade for private cars.

At present, the research on individual carbon trading mainly focuses on two aspects: The first aspect is the allocation of carbon quota. The fair allocation of carbon quota is the premise of carbon trade, and it is the main research direction. Some scholars have suggested that all adults should regularly receive an equal share of domestically free tradable quotas [4]. Fleming et al. proposed giving 40% of the cap to individuals for free and selling the remaining 60% to other energy users through bidding; equal distribution can provide incentives for every energy user, forcing them to make low-carbon behaviour [5]. However, Biran et al. believed that equal distribution is not absolutely fair, and subjective happiness is a better measure [6]. Therefore, Barns et al. proposed to auction 100% of the carbon quota to energy suppliers and distributed part of the auction revenue equally to individuals [7]. At present, the same level of fairness cannot be found. Whether it is equal distribution or auction, the policy implementation of different schemes varies greatly. For transportation, Fawcett et al. have proposed giving 50% of the carbon quota to individuals for free (including children) [8]. Wadud et al. also found that the social benefit of distribution by adults was the largest, followed by the number of cars, and the social benefit of distribution by the natural population was the worst [9]. It can be seen that the allocation of carbon quotas involving the transport sector is similar to the appeal, which is mainly free. The second aspect is the trading of carbon emission quota. It mainly revolves around carbon trade price and carbon trade mode. For carbon pricing, the Grantham Institute for Climate Change and the Environment's policy brief suggests two ways to set a carbon price. One was to consider the marginal cost of carbon emission reduction; the second was to consider the social cost of carbon [10]. For the first way, Creti et al. believed that the cost of carbon emission reduction was the least and the effect of emission reduction was the best when the carbon trade price was the same as the marginal cost of emission reduction [11]. For the second way, Wong et al. put forward the ratio of carbon emission quota to the total cost of carbon trading as a unit of carbon emission price [12]. As for carbon trade mode, Raux et al. proposed that participants bought and sold licenses through banks and other intermediary institutions or bought licenses at gas stations for carbon emissions [13]. Harwatt also proposed tradable transport carbon emission certificates to examine the carbon emissions generated by private transport in France [14].

Recently, Pan et al. proposed applying block chain technology to carbon trading to reduce the entry threshold of carbon trading market [15]. With the launch of the first block chain-based carbon exchange in Singapore, the carbon-trading model based on block chain technology has sparked a research boom among scholars. In addition, many scholars believe that carbon trading can drive the green transition. In essence, green transition is the transition of sustainable development mode oriented by ecological civilization construction [16]. For the objective, green transition is to solve the problem of harmonious coexistence between human and nature [17]. Cheng et al. showed that carbon trading cannot only reduce carbon dioxide emissions, but also has the synergistic effect of reducing SO2 and NOx emissions [18]. Through experimental research, Li et al. found that the implementation of individual carbon trading has a significant positive impact on people's use of battery electric vehicles [19]. Raux et al. has demonstrated that personal carbon trading can effectively change travel behaviour and thus reduce transport emissions from personal travel [20]. At present, personal carbon trading based on block chain has a good development prospect. Some scholars proposed the combination of block chain and micro-grid energy market, indicating that block chain is a qualified technology to operate a decentralized energy trading market [21]. In addition, the EU Scanergy project proposed a trade model combining block chain and personal carbon trade. The model can support distributed person-to-person direct transactions, and made it possible for small users to trade green energy directly [22]. Lu et al. believed that the unique decentralized transaction of block chain can realize the direct peer-to-peer transaction, reduced the cost of transaction subject, and improved the efficiency of carbon trade market [23]. Hua et al. proposed a block chain-based peer-to-peer trading framework, which provides potential design ideas for carbon-emission reduction policies by designing smart contracts and introducing distributed low-carbon incentive mechanisms [24]. Existing studies mainly focus on the theoretical application of block chain technology in carbon trading, and there are few studies on quantitative analysis of carbon trading. This paper conducts carbon trading simulation experiment based on big data of urban vehicle trajectory. The purpose is to quantitatively analyse the effect of carbon trading and provide ideas for the construction of private car carbon trading market.

The remainder of this paper is organized as follows. Section 2 proposes the application design of carbon trading based on block chain and establishes the allocation and trading model of private car carbon trading. Section 3 is the simulation result analysis of private car carbon trading. The conclusion and policy proposal are presented in Sect. 4.

2 Materials and Methods

2.1 Block Chain-Based Carbon Trading Application Design

Block chain technology has the characteristics of decentralization, collective maintenance, timestamp, open source programming, security and trust, quasi-anonymous transactions and so on. It can effectively solve these problems such as the lack of transparency in the early stage of carbon trading, the security of data storage, the excessive dependence on centralized management, and the information asymmetry between the two sides [25]. Based on the principle of "who emits, who pays", this paper establishes a carbon trading market to guide private car consumers to reduce emissions and obtain green benefits.

Block Chain-Based Carbon Trading Chain Architecture. In order to solve the problem of data storage, business isolation and transaction security in the transaction process, and ensure efficient operation of the block chain, this paper designs a main-side block chain architecture. Through the side chain protocol, the docking between the side chain of carbon trading financial business and the main chain of carbon trading data business is realized, which enables data clearance and financial transactions to be accounted separately, improves transaction efficiency, achieves automatic currency settlement, and ensures the security and stability of the main chain.

The data business chain of carbon trading is the main chain of blocks, on which user nodes, audit nodes and supervision nodes are created. The user node is the main body of carbon trading, which is mainly involved in sending and receiving trading information and recording trading matters. The audit node is an officially certified third-party audit institution that mainly participates in the audit of trading information. The regulatory node mainly participates in the policy formulation and compliance supervision in the process of carbon trading. The data service chain is mainly used for the clearing and storage of trading data. The financial business chain of carbon trading is a side chain, on which user nodes, financial nodes and regulatory nodes are created. The financial node mainly involves auditing the account information and payment for goods of the user node, while the financial business chain is mainly used to obtain the clearing data of the data business chain through the side chain protocol for currency settlement. Through two-way anchoring, the seller realizes the conversion of carbon credit into currency, and the buyer realizes the conversion of currency into carbon credit [26].

Framework of Carbon Trading System Based on Block Chain Technology.
Step 1. Monitor and record the driving time, mileage and fuel consumption of private cars through the Internet of Vehicles technology. Step 2. The big data of private car trajectory collected and recorded are used for deep learning through BP neural network to predict their carbon emissions and put them on the block chain platform. Step 3. By combining the recorded carbon emission forecast with the government's emission reduction ratio, the block chain distributes the set total carbon quota to each private car carbon consumer equally. Step 4. Private car carbon consumers accept carbon quotas and enter the trade based on the carbon emissions already used. The transaction nodes (sellers) with the remaining amount of carbon emissions release the transaction information (minimum selling price, expected rate of return) to the block chain platform; transaction nodes with excess carbon emissions (buyers) release transaction information (highest purchase price, expected rate of return) to the block chain platform; the two parties make matching trades. The first stage is the price determination stage (the seller's lowest selling price and the buyer's highest purchase price). The second stage is the bargaining stage (the seller's expected sell price and the buyer's expected purchase price). Step 5. Transaction match successfully; the main chain of data service connects the side chain of financial service through side chain protocol; the financial nodes push payment information to buyers and payment successes. The transaction node keep accounts for the transaction data and broadcasts the whole network; the third party audit institution checks the transaction data. If the audit is successful, the transaction completes. If the buyer fails to pay within the specified time, the transaction will be cancelled. Step 6. If transaction settlement is successful, the block chain platform stores the transaction and

other relevant data, the transaction node maintains the account book and the supervision node supervises it. Due to the storage and delay problems of block chain at the present stage, it is necessary to set iteration times and time limit when matching user carbon transactions. Upon completion of the specified time and number of iterations, the failed match is returned to the user node, and the seller can declare the price and expected rate of return again before the closing date of the trade to match again. Based on block chain, this paper constructs a carbon trading mechanism for private car use supplemented by government supervision and third-party auditing institutions. The specific process is shown in Fig. 1.

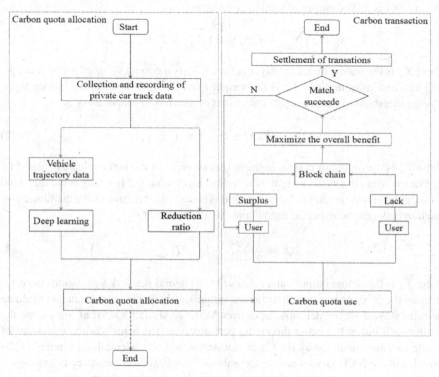

Fig. 1. Carbon trading flow chart based on block chain

2.2 Prediction of Carbon Emission and Allocation of Carbon Quota

BP Neural Network Algorithm. BP neural network is a multi-layer feed-forward network trained by error back propagation algorithm proposed by Rumelhart and McCelland in 1986. The main idea is: input learning samples and use error back propagation algorithm to adjust the weights and deviations of the network repeatedly, which makes the expected value as close as possible to the actual output value [27]. The learning rule of BP neural network is the steepest descent method. The weights and thresholds are adjusted by back propagation to minimize the sum of square error. Because BP neural network can approximate any function and has strong nonlinear mapping ability, it has become one of the most widely used artificial neural network algorithms [28]. The driving distance, driving time and driving fuel consumption in the traveling track of private cars are taken as the input layer of BP neural network, the carbon emissions of private cars are taken as the network output layer, this paper establishes a three-layer BP neural network structure to predict the carbon emissions based on private car trajectory data.

BP Neural Network Prediction Model. The number of neurons in the input layer is m, the number of neurons in the hidden layer is n, and the number of neurons in the output layer is p. The output of hidden layer neurons is:

$$X_{ij} = f\left(\sum_{i=1}^{m} W_{ij} X_i + b_j\right) \ j = 1, 2, 3, \ldots\ldots n \tag{1}$$

where X_{ij} is the output of hidden layer neurons, X_i is the input value of initial mileage, time and fuel consumption, W_{ij} is the weight from the input layer to the hidden layer, b_j is the threshold of hidden layer. The output of neurons in output layer is:

$$T_k = t\left(\sum_{1}^{n} \left(W_{jk} X_j + b_k\right)\ k = 1, 2, 3 \ldots\ldots p \tag{2}$$

where T_k Is the output of neuron in the output layer, X_j is the input value calculated by the hidden layer, W_{jk} is the weight from hidden layer to output layer, b_k is the threshold of output layer, t is the output layer function. The calculation error of the quadratic cost function between the expected output and the actual output is:

$$E = \frac{1}{2} \sum_{k=1}^{p} (Y_k - T_k)^2 \tag{3}$$

where Y_k is the actual output value. After the BP neural network simulation, the error between the predicted value and the actual output value should be evaluated to evaluate the reliability of the model, this paper uses MSE, MAE and RMSE as indicators, the smaller each index, the better the model performance. The actual carbon emissions of private cars are calculated by IPCC calculation method, the calculation formula of CO_2 provided in the IPCC Guidelines for Greenhouse Gas Emission Inventory is as follows:

$$T_{CO2} = \sum_{i=1}^{n} EF_i Q_i \tag{4}$$

where T_{co2} is the total carbon dioxide emission, Q_i is the consumption of fuel i and EF_i is the emission factor of fuel i.

Allocation of Carbon Quotas. Based on the carbon emission forecast and the government's emission reduction ratio, the total amounts of carbon quota will be equally distributed to each private car carbon consumer, this paper establishes the following model:

$$S_i = \frac{\sum_{i=1}^{m} P_{yi}}{m} \times B \tag{5}$$

where S_i is the carbon quota of the i-th private car carbon consumer, Pyi is the carbon emission forecast of the i-th private car carbon consumer, m is the number of people who get carbon quota, B is the proportion of government emission reduction. Combined with the carbon emission forecast and the government's emission reduction ratio, the period-by-period adjustment of carbon quota allocation can meet the carbon emission space required by economic growth and development, and avoid the use of constraints. In addition, the government sets the emission reduction proportion to limit the total amount of carbon emissions. Consumers with low carbon emissions can obtain relatively abundant carbon emission credits and make profits by trading abundant carbon emission credits in the market. The proportion of emission reduction set by the government is constantly adjusted with the level of economic development to meet the consumption demand of residents' daily travel.

Matching Strategy of Carbon Trading. The principle is to maximize the total profit of the transaction. The seller's lowest selling price is C_i; the buyer's highest willing purchase price is M_i. The transaction is as follows: when $C_i > M_i$, the highest willing price of the buyer is not enough to meet the price demand of the seller, and the seller refuses to trade; when $C_i \leq M_i$, the buyer's highest willing price is higher than the seller's minimum price demand, the two parties match the transaction, and transaction price $C_i \leq P_i \leq M_i$. When $P_i \leq C_i$ or $P_i \geq M_i$, the transaction fails. When the transaction matches successfully, both sides enter the bargaining stage. In essence, it is a zero sum game to divide the total transaction profit. The seller gains $P_i - C_i$ and the buyer gains $M_i - P_i$. The profit ratio of both parties to the transaction is as follows:

$$X_1 = \frac{P_i - C_i}{M_i - C_i} \tag{6}$$

$$X_2 = \frac{M_i - P_i}{M_i - C_i} \tag{7}$$

where X_1 is the return ratio of the seller, X_2 is the return ratio of the buyer ($0 \leq X_1 \leq 1, 0 \leq X_2 \leq 1$). Because the buyer and the seller have different expectations for the division of the total transaction return, X_1 is not necessarily the same as X_2. There are two cases: when $0 \leq X_1 + X_2 \leq 1$, the match is successful; when $X_1 + X_2 > 1$, the match fails. Based on the maximization of the total benefits of the transaction, this paper carries out the transaction matching according to the principle of $X_1 + X_2 = 1$. The pricing strategies of both parties are as follows:

$$P_i = C_i + X_1(M_i - C_i) \tag{8}$$

$$P_j = M_i - X_2(M_i - C_i) \tag{9}$$

$$P_n = X_1 M_i + X_2 C_i \tag{10}$$

where P_i is the seller's pricing strategy, P_j is the buyer's pricing strategy, and P_n is the successful matching transaction price. The actual benefits of carbon emissions trading between the two parties are as follows:

$$r_i = \frac{P_{max} - P_i}{P_{max}} \tag{11}$$

$$r_j = \frac{p_i - p_{min}}{p_i} \tag{12}$$

where ri is the buyer's actual rate of return, rj is the seller's actual rate of return, P_{max} is the buyer's repurchase price, and P_{min} is the seller's recovery price. In order to ensure an orderly transaction, the matching constraints during the transaction are as follows:

Carbon market trade balance can be expressed as:

$$\sum_{i=1}^{n} S_{B,i} = \sum_{j=1}^{m} S_{B,j} \tag{13}$$

where $S_{B,i}$ is the amount of carbon emissions sold by the i-th trading entity, and $S_{B,j}$ is the carbon emissions purchased by the j-th trading entity.

Carbon trading volume constraints of trading entities:

$$S_{B,i} \leq S_{Q,i} \tag{14}$$

where $S_{Q,i}$ is the total ownership of carbon emissions of the i-th trading entity.

Transaction price constraints can be expressed as:

$$C_i \leq P_i \leq M_i \tag{15}$$

$$0 \leq X_1 + X_2 \leq 1 \tag{16}$$

3   Results and Discussion

3.1   Parameter Selection

This paper selects 100000 private car trajectory data for deep learning of BP neural network. 70000 pieces of data are used to form the training set [29]. 15000 pieces of data are used to form the test set and 15000 pieces of data are used to form the validation set. The driving time, mileage and fuel consumption of private cars are taken as input variables [30]. The carbon dioxide emissions are regarded as the network output layer variable. The activation function is Sigmoid, output function is Softmax, training cycle are 1000 times, learning rate is 0.01, and training error is 10^{-6}.

3.2   Analysis of Fitting Effect

The simulation results are regressed to the real value, and the closer R is to 1, the better the fitting effect is. As can be seen from Fig. 2, training sample R = 0.99982, validation sample R = 0.99994, test sample R = 0.99989, total sample R = 0.99985. The R of all samples is greater than 0.999, and the effect is excellent [31].

As can be seen from Fig. 3, the mean square error of training set, test set and validation set converge to 10^{-6}. The error results are as follows: the mean absolute error MAE is 0.06947; the mean square error MSE is 0.01745; the root mean square error RMSE is 0.1321; the error of each sample is very small. It can be seen from the comparison

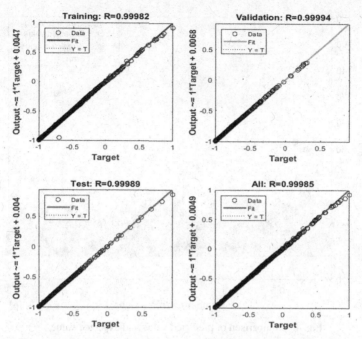

Fig. 2. Training set, validation set, test set and full sample regression curve.

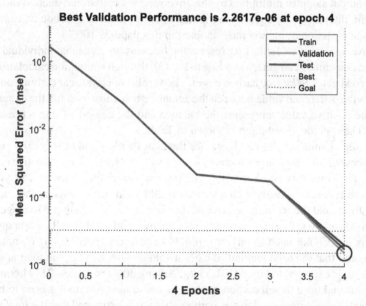

Fig. 3. Mean square error of training set, validation set and test set.

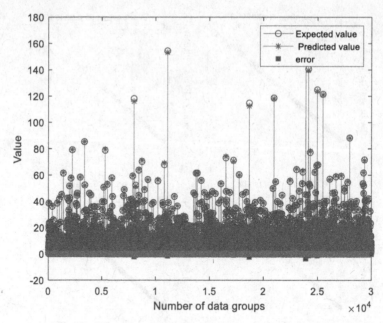

Fig. 4. Comparison of predicted value and expected value.

between the predicted value and the real value in Fig. 4, the BP neural network has excellent prediction effect. This paper takes the sum of the predicted carbon emissions of 30000 output samples multiplied by the government's emission reduction ratio as the upper limit, then it will be equally distributed to each private car carbon consumer (the government emission reduction ratio adopted in this paper is 100%).

The average quota in Table 1 represents the free carbon quota that individual private car carbon consumers can get. According to Eq. (5), through simulation calculation, each consumer can get 3.30 kg free carbon quota. The surplus of private car carbon consumers represents the difference value between the actual carbon emissions and the equalization quota. The positive value represents the balance and the negative value represents the vacancy. The specific distribution is shown in Table 1.

At present, China's carbon trading price fluctuates widely and falls year by year. The emission cost of 30–40 yuan per tonnage is too low. In order to create effective emission reduction pressure, this paper sets the guiding carbon-trading price at 250 yuan per tonnage, the recovery subsidy with a surplus is 200 yuan per tonnage at the end of the trading period, and the repurchase price of the shortage is 300 yuan per tonnage.

In 30000 samples, 21171 consumers have balance and need to sell carbon quota, 21 consumers just do not need to buy or sell, 8809 consumers need to buy carbon quota, it is estimated that the total amount of carbon sold is 43864.75 kg, the total amount of carbon quota is expected to buy 43101.55 kg. Among 30000 samples, 21171 consumers have surplus and need to sell carbon quotas, 21 consumers just do not need to buy and sell, and 8809 consumers need to buy carbon quota. It is estimated that the total amount of carbon quota sold is 43864.75 kg, and the total amount of carbon quota bought is 43101.55 kg. In this paper, normrnd function in Matlab program is used to randomly give

Table 1. Distributions and surpluses

S/N	Actual carbon emissions [kg]	Forecast carbon emissions [kg]	Quota sharing [kg]	Gap (−)/Balance (+) [kg]
1	5.07	5.05	3.30	−1.76
2	3.81	3.93	3.30	−0.50
3	5.74	5.67	3.30	−2.44
4	4.17	4.30	3.30	−0.86
5	1.20	1.23	3.30	2.11
6	0.38	0.39	3.30	2.92
7	0.34	0.35	3.30	2.97
8	1.16	1.20	3.30	2.14
9	0.12	0.11	3.30	3.18
10	0.99	1.02	3.30	2.32
11	0.67	0.69	3.30	2.64
12	2.85	2.92	3.30	0.45
...	...	...	...	...
...	...	...	...	...
30000	0.62	0.64	3.30	2.68

consumers the expected price of transaction. The mean value of the given normal distribution function is 0.25, the variance is 0.01, and the expected rate of return of consumers is $Y_i \in [0, 1]$ with 100 iterations. According to the transaction matching strategy in this paper, in this round of carbon trading, 3336 simulated transactions are matched, with a total transaction volume of 11000.62 kg. Among them, the actual transaction matching volume of seller accounted for 25.08% of the total expected sales matching volume, and the actual transaction matching volume of buyer accounted for 25.52% of the total expected purchase matching volume. A total of 29979 pieces of data are matched, and 100 iterations are performed, which take only 0.05 s. The matching strategy designed in this paper can greatly shorten the carbon trading time and improve the trading efficiency. In addition, by setting the repurchase and subsidy prices in the carbon trading market, users' trading prices will not be lower than 0.2 yuan per kg or higher than 0.3 yuan per kg. Therefore, the market can control the equilibrium of carbon trading price from the macro level, regulate the price range according to supply and demand, and guide users to recognize the deviation of price, which is conducive to the stability of carbon trading market in the early stage. The trading results are shown in Table 2.

In Table 2, the seller's lowest price (S.L) and the buyer's highest purchase price (B.H) are the upper and lower limits of the purchase price of both parties, within which the transaction can proceed. The buyer's expected price (B.E) and the seller's expected price (S.E) are the expected selling prices of both parties. The buyer's rate of return (B.R) and the seller's rate of return (S.R) are the actual rates of return obtained by both parties

Table 2. Transaction quantity table

S/N	S.L [yuan]	B.H [yuan]	S.E [yuan]	B.E [yuan]	S.R [%]	B.R [%]	T.P [yuan]	T.N [kg]	D.N [kg]	T.E [yuan]
1	0.228	0.237	0.23	0.231	13.14	23.25	0.23	172.61	80	39.74
2	0.233	0.246	0.24	0.242	16.94	19.73	0.241	147.8	40	35.53
3	0.234	0.245	0.235	0.24	15.72	20.9	0.237	508.5	247	120.67
4	0.235	0.261	0.238	0.24	16.28	20.37	0.239	566.64	189	135.37
5	0.236	0.25	0.237	0.246	17.22	19.47	0.242	595.67	305	143.91
6	0.237	0.258	0.239	0.248	17.8	18.9	0.243	769.52	248	187.2
7	0.24	0.269	0.257	0.266	23.59	12.75	0.262	416.14	77	108.92
8	0.24	0.248	0.241	0.243	17.36	19.33	0.242	671.37	332	162.47
9	0.244	0.246	0.245	0.245	18.4	18.3	0.245	1543.51	290	378.31
10	0.245	0.262	0.248	0.255	20.57	16.07	0.252	1054.53	108	265.53
11	0.245	0.254	0.248	0.253	20.13	16.53	0.25	571.26	339	143.04
12	0.247	0.249	0.248	0.249	19.42	17.27	0.248	1570.07	354	389.69
13	0.248	0.26	0.258	0.259	22.54	13.93	0.258	1144.98	213	295.63
14	0.248	0.253	0.249	0.25	19.76	16.92	0.249	587.6	364	146.46
15	0.248	0.25	0.249	0.249	0	0	0.249	0	0	0
16	0.257	0.263	0.258	0.262	23.08	13.33	0.26	680.68	150	176.98

in a transaction when they directly purchase or sell to the government or institutions. Transaction price (T.R) is the price at which both parties conclude a transaction and sell it. Transaction number (T.N) is the transaction matching quantity. Deal number (D.N) is the number of transactions successfully matched. Transaction expense (T.E) is the cost paid by the buyer to conclude the transaction.

It can be concluded from Table 2, the matching quantity of seller's transaction is 13838.7 kg, the successful matching quantity is 11000.62 kg, and the turnover rate is 79.49%. The matching quantity of buyer's transaction is 19197.19 kg, and the turnover rate is 57.3%. The market is in short supply and the carbon trading market is the seller's market. It can be seen that the transaction price of this round is distributed between 0.23 yuan per kg and 0.262 yuan per kg, which is in line with the price constraint of the market. Moreover, the price fluctuation trend does not exceed 12.21%, and the transaction price is stable. When a round of matching is completed, the failed matching can be matched on the trading deadline again. Therefore, the carbon trading based on block-chain can timely feedback market information, guide users to reasonably declare price and yields, promote the maximum trading volume of the carbon trading market, stabilize the market price and protect the marketization process.

The total return of the trading matching strategy in this paper is certain, both sides of the transaction declare the price and yield to enter the market and the actual profit depends on their expected yield, the transaction price is calculated in Eq. (10). The general trend is that the higher the minimum price a seller declares, the higher the actual return. The seller's declared price of group 7 was only 0.24 yuan per kg, lower than that of group 8 to 16. However, since the buyer's declared price was 0.269 yuan per kg, the transaction price of both parties was higher and the actual profit obtained was larger than that of the other groups. The lowest selling price of the seller and the highest buying price of the buyer can reasonably ensure that the transaction price is in an expected price range. In addition, both sides of the transaction enter the market according to their expected rate of return and match with the principle of maximizing the overall income. If the transaction is successful, both parties can obtain the expected profit.

According to the carbon trading data of both sides, all the matching groups gained certain gains except the 14th group, which failed to gain gains due to seller's insufficient supply quantity. In addition, from the perspective of the return rate of both buyers and sellers, the return rate declared by sellers is superior, which conforms to the seller's market principle and verifies that the market environment of this round of carbon trading is a seller's market.

From the perspective of a single buyer, when the seller offers 0.24 yuan per kg and the buyer offers 0.269 yuan per kg, the buyer's actual return rate is 12.75%, and when the buyer offers 0.248 yuan per kg, the buyer's actual return rate is 19.33%. The increase of buyer's rate of return is mainly due to the decrease of buyer's quotation. Therefore, when buying the same carbon price, the higher the quotation, the lower the actual yield. The match failure of the 15th group is mainly due to the seller gives priority to match the party with high quotation, and the buyer's quotation does not meet the market demand. If the seller does not enter the next round of matching before the trading day ends, it cannot obtain profits.

In Fig. 5, the buyer's actual rate of return is the rate of return that the buyer can get from participating in the carbon trading, compared with the buyer's direct repurchase from the government or institutions. The seller's actual rate of return is the rate of return that the seller can get from participating in the carbon trading, compared with the seller's direct sell from the government or institutions. The buyer's declared rate of return and the seller's declared rate of return are the rate of return that both parties intend to obtain in carbon price declaration based on the maximization of their own interests.

In terms of the actual return rate obtained by both sides of this round of transaction, except for the failure of the 15th group, both parties of the remaining groups obtain certain benefits. When the seller's quotation increases, the actual rate of return obtained by the seller generally increases. When the buyer's quotation decreases, the buyer's actual rate of return generally increases. It can be seen that the actual rate of return obtained by both parties is directly related to the declared price. The transaction cost of this round is 2729.49 yuan, compared with the direct repurchase carbon quota of 0.3 yuan per kg, the transaction cost decrease by 570.7 yuan, actual transaction costs are reduced by 17.29%, compared with the direct purchase of 0.25 yuan per kg, the carbon emission can be reduced by 2,282.8 kg. Therefore, according to the market principle of "who emits, who pays", the trading match between the two parties can reduce carbon-trading costs, reduce carbon emissions, and reflect the guiding role of carbon trading on carbon emission reduction.

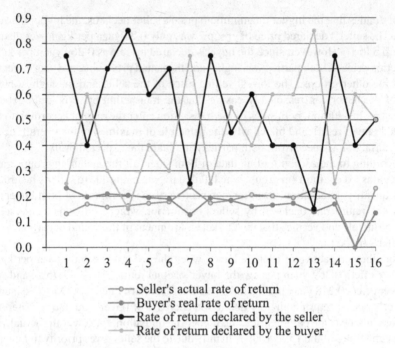

Fig. 5. Rate of return on both sides of the transaction.

In general, the buyer will lower the maximum purchase price and the seller will raise the minimum purchase price, assuming both parties want to make more profit. The zero-sum game between the two parties based on the principle of profit maximization will inevitably lead the transaction price to the market-guiding price. The transaction matching strategy in this paper can reasonably guide the transaction main body to make market offer and stabilize the market price. In addition, users can carry out multiple rounds of matching and declare the price within the trading deadline, which can reasonably guarantee the trading volume of the carbon market and stabilize the operation of the carbon trading market.

Block chain is a shared ledger of distributed data storage, characterized by decentralization, traceability and open transaction data, which can provide an open and transparent trading environment for participants in the carbon trading market [32]. This paper builds green transition driven carbon trading based on the block chain technology, embeds rules such as carbon quota allocation and carbon emissions trading into the block chain platform in the form of smart contract and provides open and transparent trading process to promote the establishment of carbon trade market.

4 Conclusions

Based on the big data of urban vehicle trajectory and combined with block chain technology, this paper proposes a carbon trading market mechanism for private cars that maximizes the benefits of both sides of the transaction, and uses the decentralized and traceable characteristics of block chain to build an open and transparent carbon trading market. It can guide private car carbon consumers to enter the market, reduce carbon dioxide emissions, and advocate green travel. In addition, through the simulation of private car consumers' personal trading, it is verified that the personal carbon trading method proposed in this paper can bring benefits to low-carbon emitters and reduce carbon emissions at the same time.

In this paper, the block chain is incorporated into the whole system of personal carbon quota allocation and carbon emission trading, and the simulation design is carried out to quantitatively analyze the emission reduction effect of carbon trading, which provides some ideas for the establishment of individual carbon trading market.

The green and low-carbon transition strategy needs to be implemented in order to achieve carbon neutralization in 2060. Based on the carbon trading mechanism proposed in this paper, relevant policy proposals can start from the following aspects. First, set higher targets for carbon emission reduction. Based on limiting the total amount of carbon emissions, per capita carbon quota should be reduced to increase the cost of carbon emissions, so as to encourage people to carry out green travel and reduce carbon emissions. Second, promote the construction of private car carbon trading market and clear private car carbon trading market positioning. The establishment of private automobile carbon trading market can stimulate the development of new energy automobile industry, restrain the negative externalities of carbon emissions of traditional fossil energy industry, thus adjust the energy structure and improve energy efficiency. In addition, we should define the positioning of the carbon trading market for private cars, build a unified carbon trading market for private cars, and make systematic arrangements in carbon quota allocation and trading to reduce carbon emissions with high efficiency. Third, formulate relatively balanced carbon emission reduction measures. Different regions in China differ greatly in economic development and energy structure, so relevant policies and measures should be formulated in light of local conditions.

Acknowledgments. This study was supported by low-carbon Transition Path and Policy Mix Innovation based on Green Governance, National Social Science Foundation of China (Grants No. 19CGL043).

References

1. Zhang, Y.: Research on China's regional carbon emission quota allocation in 2030 under the constraint of carbon intensity. Math. Probl. Eng. **2020**, 1–15 (2020)
2. Energy Foundation China: Synthesis Report 2020 on China's Carbon Neutrality: China's New Growth Pathway: from the 14th Five Year Plan to Carbon Neutrality. Energy Foundation China, Beijing, China (2020). https://www.efchina.org/Reports-en/report-lceg-20201210-en
3. IEA: World Energy Outlook 2019. IEA, Paris (2019). https://www.iea.org/reports/world-energy-outlook-2019
4. Darrell, B.: Cap and Share: A Fair Way to Cut Greenhouse Gas Emissions. The Foundation for the Economics of Sustainability (2008)
5. Fleming, D.: Energy and the Common Purpose: Descending the Energy Staircase with Tradable Energy Quotas (TEQs). The Lean Economy Connection, London (2007)

6. Biran, B.N., Shiftan, Y.: Towards a more equitable distribution of resources: using activity-based models and subjective well-being measures in transport project evaluation. Transp. Res. Part A Policy Pract. **94**, 672–684 (2016)
7. Barns, P.: Who Owns the Sky?: Our Common Assets and the Future of Capitalism. Island Press, Washington DC (2003)
8. Fawcett, T.: Carbon rationing and personal energy use. Energy Environ. **15**(6), 1067–1084 (2004)
9. Wadud, Z.: Personal tradable carbon permits for road transport: why, why not and who wins? Transp. Res. Part A **45**(10), 1052–1065 (2011)
10. Bowen, A.: The case for carbon pricing. The Grantham Research Institute in Climate Change and the Environment, Policy Brief (2011)
11. Creti, A., Jouvet, P., Mignon, V.: Carbon price drivers: Phase I versus Phase II equilibrium? Energy Econ. **34**(1), 327–334 (2012)
12. Wong, P., Chan, R.: Is carbon tax an effective driver of carbon reduction strategies adoption? Energy Policy **11**(9), 112–121 (2013)
13. Raux, C., Marlot, G.: A system of tradable CO_2 permits applied to fuel consumption by motorists. Transp. Policy **12**(3), 255–265 (2005)
14. Harwatt, H.: Reducing Carbon Emissions from Personal Road Transport through the Application of a Tradable Carbon Permit Scheme: Empirical Findings and Policy Implications from the UK. International Transport Forum, Leipzig (2008)
15. Pan, Y.T., et al.: Application of block chain in carbon trading. Energy Procedia **158**, 4286–4291 (2019)
16. Yun, R.S., Li, C.L., Li, N., Khan, M.A., Sun, X.R., Khaliq, N.: Can mixed-ownership reform drive the green transformation of SOEs? Energies **14**(10), 2964 (2021)
17. Moghaddam, H.: Carbon-netral or green LNG: a pathway toward energy transition. Pipeline Gas J. **248**(4), 54–55 (2021)
18. Cheng, B.B., Dai, H.C., Wang, P., Zhao, Q.D., Masui, T.: Impacts of carbon trading scheme on air pollutant emissions in Guangdong Province of China. Energy Sustain. Dev. **27**, 174–185 (2015)
19. Li, W.B., et al.: Would personal carbon trading enhance individual adopting intention of battery electric vehicles more effectively than a carbon tax? Resour. Conserv. Recycl. **149**, 638–645 (2019)
20. Raux, C., Croissant, Y., Pons, D.: Would personal carbon trading reduce travel emissions more effectively than a carbon tax. Transp. Res. Part D-transport Environ. **35**, 72–83 (2015)
21. Tai, X., Sun, H.B., Guo, Q.L.: Electricity transactions and congestion management based on blockchain in energy internet. Power System Technol. **40**(12), 3630–3638 (2016)
22. Zhao, Y.H., Peng, K., Xu, B.Y., Liu, Y.G.: Status and Prospect of energy blockchain application engineering. Power Syst. Autom. **43**(7), 14–22 (2019)
23. Lu, S.N., Yan, Y., Ding, Q., Wen, F.S., Zhao, J.H.: Application of blockchain in energy Internet: advantages, scenarios and cases. Zhejiang Electr. Power **36**(3), 1–4 (2017)
24. Hua, W., Jiang, J., Sun, H., Jianzhong, W.: A blockchain based peer-to-peer trading framework integrating energy and carbon markets. Appl. Energy **279**, 115539 (2020). https://doi.org/10.1016/j.apenergy.2020.115539
25. Wang, H.B.: Overview of block chain technology and application. Sci. Tech. Innov. Guide **17**(14), 126–127 (2020)
26. Ji, B., Liu, Y., Zhu, L.Y., Chang, L., Cao, B.: Design of power carbon trading mechanism based on alliance block chain. Huadian Technol. **42**(8), 32–40 (2020)
27. Goodfellow, I., Bengio, Y., Courville, A.: Deep Learning, vol. 1, pp. 326–366. MIT Press, Cambridge (2016)
28. Ma, G.H., Niu, C.L., Wang, Y.: Research on sound source location algorithm based on neural network. Digital Technol. Appl. **39**(7), 106–109 (2021)

29. Xiao, Z., et al.: TrajData: on vehicle trajectory collection with commodity plug-and-play OBU devices. IEEE Internet of Things J. **7**(9), 9066–9079 (2020)
30. Xiao, Z., Chen, Y.X., Alazab, M., Chen. H.Y.: Trajectory data acquisition via private car positioning based on tightly-coupled GPS/OBD integration in urban environments. IEEE Trans. Intell. Transp. Syst. (2021). https://doi.org/10.1109/TITS.2021.3105550
31. Huang, Y.R., Xiao, Z., Yu, X.Y., Wang, D., Havyarimana, V., Bai, J.: Road network construction with complex intersections based on sparsely-sampled private car trajectory data. ACM Trans. Knowl. Discov. Data **13**(3), 1–28 (2019)
32. Omer, F.C., Onur, C., Adnan, O.: A taxonomy for Block chain based distributed. Storage technologies. Inf. Process. Manag. **58**(5) (2021)

Matching with Externalities for Device Assignment in IoT Sharding Blockchain

Jingrou Wu[ID] and Jin Zhang[✉][ID]

Southern University of Science and Technology, Shenzhen 518055, China
11960005@mail.sustech.edu.cn, zhangj4@sustech.edu.cn

Abstract. Blockchain technology provides a powerful platform to record and manage Internet-of-Things (IoT) data. To support massive amounts of IoT data, sharding protocols are applied to enlarge the blockchain system scalability and increase efficiency. It divides the IoT devices into several committees (also called shards) so that data of different IoT devices can be processed at the same time in various shards. Random device assignment is the most popular way in IoT sharding blockchain system. Such assignment does not consider the features of different IoT devices and relationship among each IoT device. Hence, the random device assignment might lower the data processing speed. In this paper, we address this issue by modeling the IoT device assignment problem as a many-to-one matching model. Devices are assigned to only one shard while a shard can house many devices. Due to dynamic preference lists of devices, we consider the matching model with externalities. We propose an algorithm to find a stable matching and prove its convergence and stability. The simulation results indicate that the algorithm converges efficiently. Besides, the proposed algorithm has better performance than random assignment.

Keywords: Internet of Things (IoT) · Sharding blockchain · Matching theory

1 Introduction

Blockchain takes an important role in the Internet of Things (IoT) scenario [5] because it is an anonymous, traceable and secure decentralized system. However the low throughput and poor scalability becomes the bottleneck for blockchain systems. For example, Bitcoin [14] can only process 7 transactions per second (tps) and Ethereum [18] can only achieve a low speed of 13 tps [2]. The low efficiency becomes a huge challenge in IoT blockchain applications.

To address the above issue, sharding [11] technique is proposed. It divides the whole blockchain nodes into smaller groups, called committees or shards. Transactions are split into several sets and assigned to different shards. Each shard processes transactions in disjoint sets at parallel, hence increasing the throughput. As more nodes join in the sharding blockchain system, the number of shards

K. Wu et al. (Eds.): ICECI 2021, LNICST 437, pp. 46–60, 2022.
https://doi.org/10.1007/978-3-031-04231-7_4

increases accordingly which improves scalability. With the help of sharding, these new systems such as *OmniLedger* [9], *RapidChain* [19] and *Zilliqa* [1] are able to achieve processing speed thousands times higher than traditional blockchain systems.

In an IoT sharding blockchain system, blockchain nodes are firstly divided into different shards and then IoT devices, i.e., blockchain accounts, are assigned into these shard. IoT would generate data locally or transfer data to other devices. We call the recorded data as transactions in the IoT blockchain system. There are two kinds of transactions, intra-shard transactions whose input and output are in the same shard and inter-shard transactions whose input and output are in different shards. Inter-shard transactions cost more than intra-shard transactions because they require more verification and communications between involved shards. They become the main bottleneck of sharding blockchain efficiency. A sophisticated devices assignment can reduce the amount of inter-shard transactions. However, most sharding blockchain systems just simply use the random devices assignment. The random assignment algorithm does not consider the relationship between accounts. For example, it is better to assign the pair of accounts which share more transactions than others into the same shard to decrease an amount of inter-shard transactions. On the other hand, it does not take preferences of accounts over shards into consideration, leaving no room for devices to select. For example, shard size is an important factor to affect preferences of accounts. A large shard size indicates higher security than a small one when the number of malicious nodes are constant. But the large shard size decreases processing efficiency due to more communications and verification. Some accounts prefer security than efficiency while others think highly of efficiency.

The work [15] consider the transaction placement in a sharding blockchain system. It proposes a graph partition algorithm to solve transactions placement problem. However, it considers the unspent transaction outputs (UTXO) model of the sharding systems which is different from the account model we used in the IoT sharding blockchain system. UTXO model is not suitable for an IoT system because there is no such thing as the unspent transactions in the IoT system.

In this paper, we propose a new account assignment algorithm based on matching theory in IoT sharding blockchain systems which considers the features of the shards and accounts. Matching is applied in a distributed system where participants have preference over others. In our account assignment problem, both accounts and shards have preference over each other. They also want to make their decisions instead of a centralized algorithm because they have private preference information. The nature of account assignment imply that accounts are only able to select one shard but shards can hold many accounts. Besides, accounts' preferences over shards change with other accounts' choices which specify the feature of externalities. Therefore, we model such account assignment problem as a many-to-one matching game with externalities. Our contributions are as follows.

- We model the accounts assignment problem as a many-to-one matching game with externalities. This matching model also consider several constraints from the view of accounts, such as the shard size and the processing efficiency of shards.
- Then we propose an iterative algorithm to find a stable matching in which no one would like to change their actions. We also prove the convergence and stability of the algorithm.
- Our simulation results show that the proposed algorithm reach convergence quickly. Moreover, it performs better than the random assignment algorithm in reducing inter-shard transactions and achieving higher social welfare.

The rest of the paper is organized as follows. We introduce the background knowledge of sharding blockchain systems and fundamentals of matching in Sect. 2. Section 3 presents the system model and problem formulation. In Sect. 4, the algorithm for stable matching and relative proof are given. Experiment results are shown in Sect. 5, followed by related work in Sect. 6. Section 7 summarizes the work.

2   Background

In this section, we describe background knowledge of sharding blockchain and matching theory.

2.1   Sharding Blockchain

The blockchain is a decentralized system where each nodes keep a replica of the state of network. The key idea of sharding is to partition a large amount of objects into smaller subsets. In a sharding blockchain, there are three layers of sharding.

- **Network sharding.** The blockchain nodes are divided into several groups called shards or committees. Nodes would communicate with others to confirm colleagues in the same shard. Each shard is responsible to generate their own block. The block of a particular shard only need verification of nodes in the same shard instead of all participants in the system. Therefore the shard size significantly affects performance. More nodes in the same shard lead to more communication cost, therefore slowing transaction processing speed. On the other hand, a large shard size requires more malicious nodes to initiate valid affect which makes the shard much securer.
- **State sharding.** State sharding is storage partition. That is, nodes in shard A only have information about shard A instead of the whole blockchain. Not all sharding blockchains apply it such as [11]. But state sharding alleviates nodes' storage shortage and therefore improve scalability.
- **Transaction/Account sharding.** Transactions or accounts need partition as well so that they can be processed in different shards parallel. This generates two types of transactions, inter-shard transactions and intra-shard transactions. The inputs and outputs of Inter-shard transactions are in different

shards, while the inputs and outputs of intra-shard transactions are in the same shard. It is simply to process an intra-shard transaction just in the way of blockchain systems without sharding. However, it needs more design to deal with an inter-shard transactions, especially in a state sharding blockchain system. When an inter-shard transaction is sent to the shard A, usually the shard contains the outputs of the transaction, the shard A firstly find the shard B recording inputs of the transaction. Then shard A requires shard B to send verification. Only after receiving verification of shard B, shard A is able to verify and record the transaction. Hence, the inter-shard transaction incurs routing cost and communication overhead. Even worse, there are more than 95% inter-shard transactions [9,19] with the increase of blockchain size.
To further improve sharding blockchain systems efficiency, inter-shard transactions should be reduced. However, most sharding blockchain systems just assign transactions and accounts randomly.

To propose a new assignment algorithm, we need to specify the record-keep model. There are two kinds of record-keep models.

- **UTXO model.** UTXO model is applied in earlier blockchain systems such as BitCoin [14]. Instead of the user's balance, the UTXO model tracks all unspent transactions of the user. The user's balance is the sum of all unspent transactions. Such complex model allows parallel transactions cause the user could use several different UTXO simultaneously. It also provides higher privacy-protection.
- **Account model.** Account model is much simpler. It is similar with bank account which only records the account's balance. Thanks to simplicity, this model is widely used in blockchain systems with smart contract such as Ethereum [18]. On the other hand, it also improve the verification efficiency cause there is no need to follow all UTXO. Blockchain applications [10,13,17] usually use smart contract to implement more functions.

The assignment algorithms are different in this two record-keep models. In the UTXO model, transactions are assigned into shards one by one in streaming. Hence, the assignment algorithm would run at each time when a new transaction is initiated. However, in the account model, old accounts are assigned into different shards together with the process of shard formulation. The algorithm only run when a new account is created which has lower frequency than new transactions. That is, the assignment algorithm in account model has better efficiency than the algorithm in UTXO model.

2.2 Matching Theory

Matching theory is firstly proposed in [7]. It includes single-sided matching and two-sided matching. Single-sided matching studies the mapping relationship from a set to itself. For example, the roommates assignment in schools is a single-sided matching where students match with other students. Two-sided matching focuses on the mapping relationship between two disjoint sets such

as males and females, students and colleges, students and courses. The participants have their own preferences list over potential matching agents, i.e., other
participants in single-sided matching models or the members of the opposite set
in two-sided matching models. For example, students have preferences over colleges which might base on the colleges' reputation, the major and other factors.
Similarly, colleges also rank students in their preferences.

We introduce more details of two-sided matching models following because it
is the model we used in this paper. We call the two-sided matching as "matching"
for short in following paper. According to the mapping relationships, there are
three kinds of matching models.

– **One-to-one Matching.** Each agent of the set is able to match one agent of
  the other set. Marriage is a typical application of one-to-one matching where
  one person is supposed to marry another one.
– **Many-to-one Matching.** The members of the one set are allowed to have
  multiple relationships with agents of the other set while the participants of
  the other set only matches with the only one agents of the set. The matching
  between students and colleges is a many-to-one matching where a student
  can be admitted into only one college while a college has many students.
– **Many-to-Many Matching.** Agents of each set can hold many participants
  of the other set. For example, a student can choose many courses while the
  course is open to many students as well.

We could also divide the matching model into two types based on participants' preference lists.

– **Matching without externalities.** In this matching model, participants'
  preference lists keep same for all time. They would not change their preference
  lists for any reason.
– **Matching with externalities.** Different from the above model, the preference list of each participant would change due to externalities. For example,
  a student might be more likely to go to a college when her best friend also
  applies to it. Hence, the preference list of this student is dynamic over her
  best friend's choice.

Stable matching takes an important part in matching models. The stable
matching means that there does not exists a pair of agents who prefer each
other than their current selections. Hence, they would not leave current pair and
the matching remains same. The deferred acceptance (DA) algorithm is proposed
in [7] to find a stable matching. It is useful for matching without externalities.
However, in a matching with externalities model, the DA algorithm is not always
able to find a stable matching due to dynamic preference lists. A weaker stable
matching, i.e. two-sided exchange stable or swap stable, is defined in [4].

3   System Model and Problem Formulation

We consider an account mode instead of UTXO mode sharding blockchain in
our system because account mode is more widely used. We regard the account
assignment as a one-shot process at the beginning of each epoch.

3.1   Shards and Accounts Model

The blockchain system is comprised of N shards denoted by $S = \{s_1, s_2, ..., s_N\}$. Each shard s_i has m_i miners. The total transaction capacity of each shard is different, presented by c_i. We assume all miners are rational and they share the same rewards as long as they are colleagues. Therefore, the miners in the identical shard would always make the consistent decision to maximize their rewards. In this way, We can regard the shard as a rational participant instead of a set of miners for simplicity.

We assume M accounts $A = \{a_1, a_2, ..., a_M\}$ need assigned at the time. An account belongs to only one shard while a shard can hold several accounts in an epoch. Each account a_j has n_j transactions to be processed in the following epoch and the average transaction fee is r_j. A graph $G \doteq (V, E, W)$ is used to model the detail information of transactions where node set $V = \{a_1, a_2, ..., a_M\}$ is the set of accounts and the edge set $E = \{(a_{j_1}, a_{j_2})|j_1 \neq j_2\}$ is the set of transactions. The number of transactions between each accounts is denoted by $W = \{w_{j_1,j_2}|j_1 \neq j_2\}$ where w_{j_1,j_2} is the transaction amount between account j_1 and j_2. For simplify, we assume the graph is an undirected graph which means there are total w_{j_1,j_2} transactions between a_{j_1} and a_{j_2}. The edge (a_{j_1}, a_{j_2}) and (a_{j_2}, a_{j_1}) are identical and $w_{j_1,j_2} = w_{j_2,j_1}$. We also define the set of accounts who have transactions with the account a_j as $T(a_j) = \{a_k|w_{j,k} > 0\}$. Then the relative accounts in the same shard of the account a_j is $T(a_j, s_i) = \{a_k|w_{jk} > 0 \, and \, a_k \in s_i\}$ where $a_k \in s_i$ means the account a_k is assigned to the shard s_i. So the inter-shard relative accounts of the account a_j are in the set $T(a_j)\backslash T(a_j, s_i)$.

3.2   Problem Formulation

Given the shards and accounts model, we formulate the problem as an optimal accounts assignment. We introduce the constraints of the system and give the formulation detail in this subsection.

Accounts Preference. Accounts rank the shard from three aspects as follows.

- **Shard size.** Each account a_j has the minimum and maximum number of the shard's miners, denoted by $m_{j_{min}}$ and $m_{j_{max}}$ because the shard size affects the consensus efficiency and security. If the shard size is not in this range, the account would not consider the shard. The preference of the account a_j on the shard s_i size, denoted by $\pi_s^{a_j}(m_i)$.
- **Transaction processing ability.** Transaction processing ability is relative with the remain transaction capacity. Accounts are more willing to join in a shard with sufficient room for transactions because it is more likely to have transactions serviced. The effect of remain capacity $\pi_c^{a_j}(c_i)$ is an increasing function with the remain capacity c_i of the shard s_i.
- **Neighbour accounts.** Accounts prefer intra-shard transactions than inter-shard transactions and therefore, they would like to stay in a shard with more relative accounts. We use $\pi_n^{a_j}(T(a_j, s_i))$ to describe such preference.

To give a shard an overall rank, the account a_j also has weight parameters $\omega_{1j}, \omega_{2j}, \omega_{3j}$ to combine these three preferences together. Accounts select shards by overall rank consisting of the shard's size, transaction processing speed and accounts in the same shard. Different accounts have different thoughts on these aspects as well. Hence, the utility of the account a_j to choose the shard s_i is defined as follows:

$$
\begin{aligned}
u_{a_j}(s_i) &= \omega_{1_j} \pi_s^{a_j}(m_i) + \omega_{2_j} \pi_p^{a_j}(c_i) + \omega_{3_j} \pi_n^{a_j}(T(a_j, s_i)) \\
&= \omega_{1_j}(m_i - x_j)^2 + \omega_{2_j} c_i \\
&+ \omega_{3_j} \sum_{a_k \in T(a_j, s_i)} w_{a_j, a_k}.
\end{aligned}
\tag{1}
$$

The weights $\omega_{1_j}, \omega_{2_j}, \omega_{3_j}$ can be different for various accounts.

Shards Preference. Shards only consider the benefit brought by the account. The utility is composed of transaction fees $R(A_i) = \sum_{a_j \in A_i} n_j r_j$ and processing cost $C(A_i)$ where A_i is the account set of the shard s_i. The cost of dealing with these transactions is divided into two parts, the intra-shard cost and the inter-shard cost. We define the cost of each intra-shard transaction as c_i and the cost of each inter-shard transaction as c_c. As mentioned above, intra-shard transactions cost less than inter-shard transactions. Hence we have $c_i < c_c$. The total cost of the set A_i is the sum of all intra-shard transaction cost and inter-shard transaction cost,

$$
\begin{aligned}
C(A_i) = &\frac{1}{2} \sum_{a_j \in A_i} \sum_{a_{k_1} \in V(a_j, s_i)} c_i w_{jk_1} \\
&+ \frac{1}{2} \sum_{a_j \in A_i} \sum_{a_{k_2} \in \bigcup_{k \neq i} V(a_j, s_k)} c_c w_{jk_2}.
\end{aligned}
\tag{2}
$$

Therefore the utility of the shard s_i containing the set of accounts A_i is

$$
u_{s_j}(A_i) = R(A_i) - C(S_i).
\tag{3}
$$

Accounts Assignment Problem. Given the preferences of accounts and shards, we aim to maximize shards utility with accounts requirements as follows:

$$
\max_{A_i} \qquad u_{s_j}(A_i) = R(A_i) - C(S_i)
\tag{4a}
$$

$$
s.t. \qquad x_{j_{min}} \leq m_i \leq x_{j_{max}}, \forall a_j \in S_i
\tag{4b}
$$

$$
v_j \leq v_i(S_i), \forall a_j \in S_i
\tag{4c}
$$

where constraint 4b means that the account a_j is only willing to choose a shard with proper number of miners and constraint 4c indicates that the process speed of the shard i must satisfies all accounts' requirements.

4 Many-to-One Matching for Accounts Assignment

In this section, we firstly give the formal definition of many-to-one matching for accounts assignment and then propose an algorithm to solve this matching problem.

4.1 Accounts Assignment Matching Model

We apply the many-to-one matching model in the shards and accounts where a shard holds many accounts and an account belongs to the only one shard. The formal definition is given as follows.

Definition 1 (Many-to-one matching). *Given the set of accounts $A = \{a_1, a_2, ..., a_M\}$ and the set of shards $S = \{s_1, s_2, ..., s_N\}$, the many-to-one matching μ is a mapping: $A \cup S \cup \{\emptyset\} \rightarrow 2^A \cup (S \times 2^A \cup \{\emptyset, \emptyset\})$, satisfying following conditions:*

1. *$\mu(a_j) \in S \times A_{a_j} \cup \{\emptyset, \emptyset\}$, for all $a_j \in A$ where A_{a_j} is the subset of A containing a_j.*
2. *$\mu(s_i) \in 2^A$, for all $s_i \in S$.*
3. *$\mu(\emptyset) = \emptyset$.*
4. *if $a_j \in \mu(s_i)$, then $\mu(a_j) = (s_i, \mu(s_i))$.*
5. *if $\mu(a_j) = (s_i, A')$, then $\mu(s_i) = A'$.*

The first three conditions indicate the matching results of accounts and shards. The matching result of an account is a combination of the selected shard and neighbouring accounts, i.e., accounts in the same shard, as the condition 1 shows. It also means that the account is assigned to only one shard. The special case here is $\mu(a_j) = \{\emptyset, \emptyset\}$ which means that the account a_j is not matched to any shard. The condition 2 describes the matching result of a shard where the shard contains a subset of accounts. As for the empty set, the condition 3 define the mapping result as the empty set as shows. The last two conditions 4 and 5 specify the properties of matching. If an account is assigned to a shard, then the shard must contain this account and vice versa. For simplification, we use $\mu(a_j) = s$ where $a_j \in A$ and $s \in S \cup \{\emptyset\}$ to represent $\mu(a_j) = (s, \mu(s))$.

In a matching model, preferences take an important role. Both shards and accounts make decisions based on their preferences. The utilities measure the preferences of shards and accounts as the Eq. (4a) and Eq. (1) show. We define the reflexive, transitive and complete binary relationship $\succ$ between preference relationship. The preference over accounts of the shard s_i is denoted by $\succ_{s_i}$ and similarly, the preference over shards of the account a_j is presented by $\succ_{a_j}$.

Definition 2 (Preference over accounts of shards). *For all $A_{a_i}, A_{a_i'}(a_i \neq a_{i'}) \in 2^A$ and $s_i \in S$, $A_i \succ_{s_i} A_i'$ if and only if $u_{s_i}(A_{a_i}) > u_{s_i}(A_{a_{i'}})$.*

Definition 3 (Preference over shards of accounts). *For all $s_i, s_{i'}(s_i \neq s_{i'}) \in S$ and $a_j \in A$, $(s_i, \mu(s_i)) \succ_{a_j} (s_{i'}, \mu(s_{i'}))$ if and only if $u_{a_j}(s_i) > u_{a_j}(s_{i'})$.*

Shards and accounts are able to establish the preference list by ranking the utility. Shards do not consider matching results of other shards while accounts care about their neighbouring accounts in the same shard. Hence, it becomes a many-to-one matching model with externalities. That is, the preference lists of accounts are dynamic which changes with other accounts states.

Due to externalities, the traditional stable matching is hard to find. Instead, the concept of two-sided exchange-stable [4] is applied in such matching model. The two-sided exchange-stable matching bases on the concept of swap matching.

Definition 4 (Swap matching). *We define two kinds of swap matching as follows:*

- **Two-sided exchange.** *Given the matching μ, for any $a_j, a_{j'} \in A$ with $s_i = \mu(a_j) \neq s_i' = \mu(a_{j'})$, the swap matching $\mu_{a_j}^{a_{j'}}$ of the original matching μ with two accounts $a_j, a_{j'}$ is defined as $\mu_{a_j}^{a_{j'}} = \{\mu \backslash \{(a_j, s_i), (a_{j'}, s_i')\}\} \cup \{(a_j, s_i'), (a_{j'}, s_i)\}$.*
- **Account-vacancy exchange.** *Given the original matching μ and any account $a_j \in A$, we have $\mu(a_j) = s_i$. For any $s \in S, s \neq s_i$, the swap matching $\mu_{a_j}^{\emptyset}$ is defined as $\mu_{a_j}^s = \{\mu \backslash \{a_j, s_i\}\} \cup \{a_j, s\}$.*

Two-sided exchange defines the exchange between two accounts. In this type of swap, only two accounts in different shards exchange their positions while other accounts stay in the original shards. The second kind of swap allows an exchange between an account and an available vacancy in other shards.

Accounts and shards are not always glad to swap. We define the acceptable swap operation as swap-blocking pair.

Definition 5 (Swap-blocking pair). *According to different types of swap matching, we define two swap-blocking pair as follows.*

- **Two-sided pair.** *In a matching μ, the swap-blocking pair $(a_j, a_{j'})$ for any $a_j, a_{j'} \in A$ with $s_i = \mu(a_j) \neq s_{i'} = \mu(a_{j'})$ satisfies following three conditions.*
  1. *$u_a^{\mu_{a_j}^{a_{j'}}} \geq u_a^{\mu}$, for both accounts $a \in \{a_j, a_{j'}\}$.*
  2. *$u_{s_i}^{\mu_{a_j}^{a_{j'}}} + u_{s_{i'}}^{\mu_{a_j}^{a_{j'}}} \geq u_{s_i}^{\mu}$.*
  3. *Either one of two inequalities is strict.*
  where u_x^{μ} is the utility of the player $x \in A \cup S$ in the matching μ.
- **Account-vacancy pair.** *In a matching μ, the swap-blocking pair (a_j, s) for any $a_j \in A$ with $s_i \neq \mu(a_j) \neq s$ satisfies following three conditions.*
  1. *$u_{a_j}^{\mu_{a_j}^s} \geq u_{a_j}^{\mu}$.*
  2. *$u_{s_i}^{\mu_{a_j}^s} + u_s^{\mu_{a_j}^s} \geq u_{s_i}^{\mu} + u_s^{\mu}$.*
  3. *Either one of above inequalities is strict.*

The first condition requires non-decrease accounts utility after swap. The second condition means non-decrease total utilities of concerned shards. The last condition indicates either the accounts utility or the shards utility should increase with the swap. These three conditions are reasonable because both accounts and shards are individually rational. Accounts refuse the swap when they found the utility become less after the swap. As for shards, they care about not only themselves but also the whole blockchain system. Therefore, they would like to swap when the total utilities increase.

Then, we define two-sided exchange-stable (also called swap-stable) matching.

Definition 6 (Two-sided exchange-stable matching). *A matching μ is a two-sided exchange-stable matching if and only if no swap-blocking pair exists.*

The stable matching is important. Otherwise, either accounts or shards would like to change their current decisions.

4.2   Accounts Assignment Algorithm

In this section, we propose a naive iterative accounts assignment algorithm to find an swap-stable many-to-one matching.

- Firstly, we initiate a random matching μ_0 between accounts and shards.
- Then, we search for a swap-blocking pair in this step. Once a swap-blocking pair $(a_j, a_{j'})$ or (a_j, s) is found, we allow the swap operation. Hence, the matching becomes $\mu_{a_j}^{a_{j'}}$ or $\mu_{a_j}^{s}$ respectively.
- Repeat the above step until we find a matching μ^* without any swap-blocking pair.

We then prove the convergence and stability of the Algorithm 1.

Theorem 1 (Convergence).   *The Algorithm 1 is able to converge to the matching μ^* finally.*

Proof. From the definition of the swap-blocking pair, we know that each swap operation increases either involved accounts' utilities or the total utilities of involved shards. We set $us(\mu) = \sum_{s \in S} u_s(\mu)$. In a swap operation, utilities of all shards remain stable except for involved shards. Then sum of utilities of involved shards is non-decreasing. Hence, we have $us(\mu') \geq us(\mu)$ where μ' is the swap matching of μ. We also define $ua(\mu') = \sum_{a \in A} u_a(\mu)$.

- If $us(\mu')$ is always greater than $us(\mu)$ after each swap, then convergence is reached when $us(\mu') = us(\mu)$. Because $us(\mu)$ has maximum value, $us(\mu')$ will be equal to $us(\mu)$ in limited rounds.
- If $us(\mu') = us(\mu)$ before convergence, the two-sided exchange must happen because account-vacancy exchange must lead to $us(\mu') > us(\mu)$. In this two-sided exchange, only the accounts in two-sided exchange pair change

---

Algorithm 1. Accounts Assignment Algorithm

Input: Accounts set A, shards set S, transactions graph G
Output: The swap-stable matching μ^*
1: Randomly initialize μ
2: **repeat**
3:　　**for** $a_j \in A$ **do**
4:　　　**for** $s_i \in S$ **do**
5:　　　　**if** (a_j, s_i) is a swap-blocking pair **then**
6:　　　　　$\mu^* = \mu_{a_j}^{s_i}$
7:　　　　**end if**
8:　　　**end for**
9:　　**end for**
10:　　**for** $a_j, a_j' \in A, j \neq j'$ **do**
11:　　　**if** (a_j, a_j') is a swap-blocking pair **then**
12:　　　　$\mu^* = \mu_{a_j}^{a_j'}$
13:　　　**end if**
14:　　**end for**
15: **until** No swap-blocking pair exists

(improve) their utility while other accounts and shards remain the same utilities. Therefore, this two-sided exchange does not bring externalities and hence our algorithm would never go back to any previous state. Due to limited state space size, the algorithm would converge finally.

The Algorithm 1 would converge in both two conditions, and therefore it is able to converge to μ^* eventually.

Theorem 2 (Two-sided stability). *The matching μ^* obtained from the Algorithm 1 is two-sided stable.*

Proof. We prove this theorem by contradiction. Assuming the final matching μ^* is not two-sided stable, then there must exist a swap-blocking pair as definition 6 defines. If so, the Algorithm 1 would not terminate due to the existence of the swap-blocking pair. Hence, the matching μ^* is not the final matching from the Algorithm 1 which is contradict to the assumption.

Therefore, the Algorithm 1 output μ^* is a two-sided stable matching.

5　Experimental Results

In this section, we conduct numerical simulations of the proposed many-to-one matching model. We firstly show the efficiency of the Algorithm 1. We use simulation results to present the Theorem 1 that the Algorithm 1 convergences in limited round. Then we compare the total utilities and social welfare of the many-to-one matching model with the random algorithm.

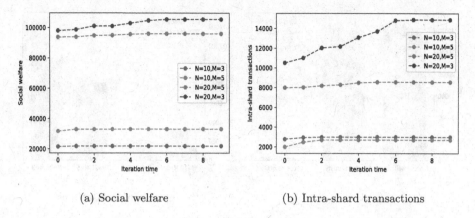

(a) Social welfare   (b) Intra-shard transactions

Fig. 1. Social welfare and the number of intra-shard transactions of iterations

5.1 Simulation Setup

Our simulation setting is as follows, unless otherwise noted.

We conduct the simulation with $N = 10$ accounts and $M = 5$ shards. The shards' capacity is randomly assigned. The number of miners in each shard is distributed from the uniform distribution $U \sim [4, 10]$. Accounts have their own perfect shard's size $x_a, a \in A$ which is drawn from the uniform distribution $U \sim [3, 11]$. Accounts accept the shard's size lying on $[x_a - \epsilon, x_a + \epsilon]$ where ϵ is set to be 2. Accounts' preference weights are generated randomly.

As for the transaction graph, we firstly specify the degree of busyness for each account. Based on the busyness, we create transactions and build a graph. We assume in the next epoch, accounts would not initiate more than 100 transactions.

5.2 Convergence Efficiency

In Fig. 1(a) and 1(b), we show the convergence of the Algorithm 1 with different amount of accounts and shards, i.e. $N = 10$ accounts with $M = 3$ shards, $N = 10$ accounts with $M = 5$ shards, $N = 20$ accounts with $M = 3$ shards and $N = 20$ accounts with $M = 5$ shards.

As the Theorem 1 and Theorem 6 claimed, the proposed algorithm converges in limited rounds. The convergence takes palace in several rounds. There are only 2 iterations in $N = 10, M = 3$ and 3 in $N = 10, M = 5$. With $N = 20$ accounts and $M = 5$ shards, the algorithm reaches the convergence in 5 rounds. It costs 7 rounds to converge with $N = 20$ accounts and $M = 3$ shard. The iteration times increases with both number of shards and accounts because more shards and accounts bring more possible assignments.

Figure 1(a) shows the change of social welfare with iterations. We noticed that the social welfare does not always increase with iterations. Because the swap operation only considers utilities of concerned parties, other accounts might have

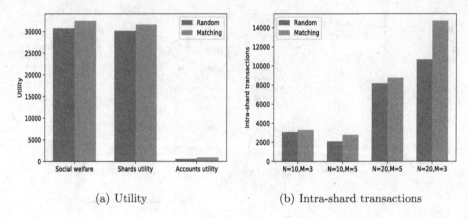

(a) Utility   (b) Intra-shard transactions

Fig. 2. Utility and intra-shard transactions in the matching algorithm and random assignment

utility decreased after swap. But we could see only one swap operation at the first iteration would increase social welfare significantly.

In Fig. 1(b), we could see the change of number of intra-shard transactions with iterations. Different from the social welfare, the intra-shard transactions in non-decreasing with iteration times. Because the swap operation would not bring more transaction fees for all transactions. It just transfer from one shard to another shard. Due to non-decreasing utilities of involved shards, the cost decreases while the income remains same. That is, there are more intra-shard transactions and less inter-shard transactions compared with the previous matching.

5.3   Compare with Random Assignment

We measure performance of the proposed algorithm in both utility improvement and intra-shard increase by comparing with the random assignment.

Figure 2(a) shows the improvement of utility with $N = 10$ accounts and $M = 5$ shards. The utilities of both shards and accounts increase by applying the proposed algorithm. Therefore, the social welfare is improved accordingly.

Figure 2(b) compare the number of intra-shard transactions in four settings. In each setting, the proposed algorithm induce more intra-shard transactions than the random assignment.

6   Related Work

Shading protocols aim to improve scalability and enhance throughput of traditional blockchain systems. Most sharding-relative works focus on sharding system design [6,9,11,19]. The concept of sharding is firstly applied in a permissioned blockchain system of the centrally bank [6]. *ELASTICO* [11] is the first perminssionless blockchain system using sharding technique. The shards are formed randomly according to miners' solutions to the hash puzzle and then accounts are assigned to shards in the same way. Similar random accounts assignment are applied in *OmniLedger* [9] and *RapidChain* [19]. Compared with the first work in sharding perminssionless blockchain system, they provide stage sharding protocols for further performance improvement.

Among these works, shards formulation and accounts assignment are introduced briefly without any sophisticated design and analysis. Random shards formulation and accounts assignment are most popular because they are easy for implementation. Shards formulation is studied in [3]. A coalition game is proposed to model the problem of reputation-based shards formulation. The new shards formulation algorithm increases the system's security and throughput. *OptiShard* [8] invests the optimal shard size in a sharding blockchain systems based on two features: performance and security. The work [15] focus on transactions placement in an UTXO sharding blockchain model. It models the transaction relationship as a graph and proposes a graph partition algorithm *OptChain* for transactions assignment. *OptChain* algorithm decreases inter-shard transactions significantly. However it is not suitable in an account model.

There are also some other works providing participants' behaviour analysis from the view of game theory. The work [12] aims to maximize participants' engagement. It provide an incentive mechanism to motivate participants' cooperation. An evolutionary game [16] is used to analysis the change of participants population in sharding applications.

None of above works leverages the matching theory for accounts assignment problem.

7   Conclusion

We investigated the devices assignment problem in an IoT sharding blockchain system. We model the devices assignment as a many-to-one matching model with externalities. We come up with an iterative algorithm to find a two-sided exchange stable matching of accounts (IoT devices) and shards in this model. We give a complete proof of the convergence and stability of the proposed algorithm. At last, we evaluate the matching model and the algorithm to show its convergence efficiency and better performance. Compared with the random assignment, our mechanism increases total utilities of shards and social welfare.

Acknowledgement. This work was supported in part by the National Natural Science Foundation of China under Grant No. 61701216, Shenzhen Science, Technology and Innovation Commission Basic Research Project under Grant No. JCYJ20180507181527806, Guangdong Provincial Key Laboratory (Grant No. 2020B121201001) and "Guangdong Innovative and Entrepreneurial Research Team Program"(2016ZT06G587) and the "Shenzhen Sci-Tech Fund"(KYTDPT20181011104007).

References

1. The zilliqa project (2017). https://www.zilliqa.com
2. Scalability-bitcoin wiki (2018). https://en.bitcoin.it/wiki/Scalability

3. Asheralieva, A., Niyato, D.: Reputation-based coalition formation for secure self-organized and scalable sharding in IoT blockchains with mobile edge computing. IEEE Internet Things J. **PP**(99), 1 (2020)
4. Bodine-Baron, E., Lee, C., Chong, A., Hassibi, B., Wierman, A.: Peer effects and stability in matching markets. In: Persiano, G. (ed.) SAGT 2011. LNCS, vol. 6982, pp. 117–129. Springer, Heidelberg (2011). https://doi.org/10.1007/978-3-642-24829-0_12
5. Conoscenti, M., Vetró, A., Martin, J.: Blockchain for the internet of things: a systematic literature review. In: The Third International Symposium on Internet of Things: Systems, Management and Security (IOTSMS-2016) (2016)
6. Danezis, G., Meiklejohn, S.: Centrally banked cryptocurrencies. arXiv preprint arXiv:1505.06895 (2015)
7. Gale, D., Shapley, L.S.: College admissions and the stability of marriage. Amer. Math. Monthly **69**(1), 9–15 (1962)
8. Kantesariya, S., Goswami, D.: Determining optimal shard size in a hierarchical blockchain architecture. In: 2020 IEEE International Conference on Blockchain and Cryptocurrency (ICBC), pp. 1–3 (2020). https://doi.org/10.1109/ICBC48266.2020.9169448
9. Kokoris-Kogias, E., Jovanovic, P., Gasser, L., Gailly, N., Syta, E., Ford, B.: OmniLedger: a secure, scale-out, decentralized ledger via sharding. In: 2018 IEEE Symposium on Security and Privacy (SP), pp. 583–598. IEEE (2018)
10. Li, M., et al.: CrowdBC: a blockchain-based decentralized framework for crowd-sourcing. IEEE Trans. Parallel Distrib. Syst. **30**(6), 1251–1266 (2019). https://doi.org/10.1109/TPDS.2018.2881735
11. Luu, L., Narayanan, V., Zheng, C., Baweja, K., Gilbert, S., Saxena, P.: A secure sharding protocol for open blockchains. In: Proceedings of the 2016 ACM SIGSAC Conference on Computer and Communications Security, pp. 17–30 (2016)
12. Manshaei, M.H., Jadliwala, M., Maiti, A., Fooladgar, M.: A game-theoretic analysis of shard-based permissionless blockchains. IEEE Access **6**, 78100–78112 (2018)
13. Montes, J.M., Ramirez, C.E., Gutierrez, M.C., Larios, V.M.: Smart contracts for supply chain applicable to smart cities daily operations. In: 2019 IEEE International Smart Cities Conference (ISC2), pp. 565–570 (2019). https://doi.org/10.1109/ISC246665.2019.9071650
14. Nakamoto, S.: A peer-to-peer electronic cash system (2008). https://bitcoin.org
15. Nguyen, L.N., Nguyen, T.D.T., Dinh, T.N., Thai, M.T.: OptChain: optimal transactions placement for scalable blockchain sharding. In: 2019 IEEE 39th International Conference on Distributed Computing Systems (ICDCS), pp. 525–535 (2019). https://doi.org/10.1109/ICDCS.2019.00059
16. Ni, Z., Wang, W., Kim, D.I., Wang, P., Niyato, D.: Evolutionary game for consensus provision in permissionless blockchain networks with shards. In: ICC 2019–2019 IEEE International Conference on Communications (ICC), pp. 1–6. IEEE (2019)
17. Pee, S.J., Kang, E.S., Song, J.G., Jang, J.W.: Blockchain based smart energy trading platform using smart contract. In: 2019 International Conference on Artificial Intelligence in Information and Communication (ICAIIC), pp. 322–325 (2019). https://doi.org/10.1109/ICAIIC.2019.8668978
18. Wood, G.: Ethereum: a secure decentralised generalised transaction ledger (2014). https://ethereum.org
19. Zamani, M., Movahedi, M., Raykova, M.: RapidChain: scaling blockchain via full sharding. In: Proceedings of the 2018 ACM SIGSAC Conference on Computer and Communications Security, pp. 931–948 (2018)

Openflow-Extended Queue Scheduling for Multi-tenants in Access Network

Ting Wang[1(✉)] and Gang Liu[2]

[1] Software Engineering Institute, East China Normal University, Shanghai, China
twang@sei.ecnu.edu.cn
[2] Bell Labs, Nokia Shanghai Bell Corp., Shanghai, China
gang.i.liu@nokia-sbell.com

Abstract. Network slicing is a mechanism that could be used by operators to support multiple virtual networks over underlying hardware infrastructure. Typically, it could leverage Network Function Virtualization (NFV) technology to share the computing/storage resources in data center scenarios, for example, creating multiple VM (virtual machine) instances for different network functions or network tenants. Through different VM instances, most of computing-intensive core network applications (e.g. vEPC, vIMS) could be supported. In order to achieve this goal, in this paper we propose a novel Openflow-extended queue scheduling scheme for multi-tenants in the access network.

Keywords: Network function virtualization · Network slicing · Queue scheduling

1 Introduction

The idea of splitting the data plane and the control plane is widely accepted. As an open interface between the control plane and data plane, OpenFlow [1] was originally proposed and developed at Stanford University [2] and is now marshalled by the Open Networking Foundation (ONF) [3]. The Software-Defined Access Network (SDAN) concept [4] was introduced to extend the benefits of Software Defined Networking (SDN) and Network Function Virtualization (NFV) into broadband access [2,5]. However, there are still many open issues to be addressed. For example, how to slice fixed access networks? As shown in Fig. 2, how to support multi-tenants sharing the same ONU as well as the link resource with access nodes? How to identify traffics of different virtual network operators (VNOs) while guaranteeing strong isolation between them? How to provide complete logical resource for each VNO without any conflict? For example, complete VLAN tags (0-4096) could be employed by each VNO.

In traditional access network, a variety of different access technologies and modes (from ADSL to VDSL, EPON to GPON) would coexist or even collocate in a quite long period. The diversity of access technologies increases the cost of

© ICST Institute for Computer Sciences, Social Informatics and Telecommunications Engineering 2022
Published by Springer Nature Switzerland AG 2022. All Rights Reserved
K. Wu et al. (Eds.): ICECI 2021, LNICST 437, pp. 61–73, 2022.
https://doi.org/10.1007/978-3-031-04231-7_5

hardware maintenance and complicates network O&M. When operators want to migrate the line access technology (for example, from ADSL to VDSL or even G.fast), they have to manually upgrade the access device (at least LT board) accordingly. Furthermore, if operators want to deploy a specialized or customized (maybe not standardized) protocol or feature, it would be quite difficult, and they will basically have to wait for vendors to produce dedicated processing boards (LT board). Due to the highly coupled hardware and software, closed and proprietary device, and standard-oriented eco-system, the telecom-specific network equipment is prone to a lack of flexibility, and the operators usually have to change the hardware (e.g. LT board) so as to support new protocols or customized features.

Moreover, currently most of the existing access networks are dedicatedly deployed by the incumbent operators, with extremely high expenditure invested on infrastructure construction and access network deployment. Greenfield or alternative operator, who wants to extend their services to the same area, must deploy their own dedicated access infrastructure networks, though in fact the infrastructure deployed by the incumbent operator is underutilized with many unused optical fibers underground as well as other access resource. This model is accompanied with various disadvantages such as the investment waste for the operators and low resource utilization. Besides, the customers are impossible to make dynamic selections among different operators, incurring high cost on manually changing the customer lines. To deal with these issues, this paper aims to achieve a virtualized access network supporting multi-tenancy and flexible slicing through queue scheduling optimization. With this aim, this paper proposes an OpenFlow-enabled queue scheduling methodology for network slicing and traffic isolation. In order to facilitate the centralized queue management, we introduce a new "Enqueuer" module in the access controller and extend OpenFlow protocol [1] to indicate queue scheduler as well as queue property.

The remainder of this paper is organized as follows. Section 2 briefly reviews the related work. Section 4 describes the basic idea of the proposed solution. Section 5 presents the design details of the solution. Section 6 concludes this paper.

2   Related Work

Currently, there is little research on fixed access network sharing, especially on how to slice the access resource between ONU and access node. The most similar case is the slicing of forwarding devices.

For those OpenFlow-enabled forwarding devices (e.g. switch, router, etc.), "FlowVisor" solution could be a feasible choice to support multi-tenants [6]. As shown in Fig. 1, FlowVisor is a special OpenFlow controller that acts as a transparent proxy between OpenFlow switches and multiple OpenFlow controllers. FlowVisor creates rich "slices" of network resources and delegates control of each slice to a different controller which may belong to different VNOs, such as Alice Controller, Bob controller, and Cathy Controller. But in the "FlowVisor" solution, the InP controller could not obtain queue-relevant information from underlying devices. It means that the InP controller has no knowledge/capability to manage the queue scheduling. To address this problem, this paper extends

OpenFlow protocol to help controller get the queue information from underlying devices. In the InP controller, specific modules are designed to perform centralized queue scheduling and enable strong isolation between different VNOs. Y. Oktian, etc. [7] investigated different design approaches of SDN controller. They classified the methods into several design choices, where each design choice may influence several SDN issues such as scalability, robustness, consistency, and privacy. They further analyzed the advantages and disadvantages of each model regarding these matters.

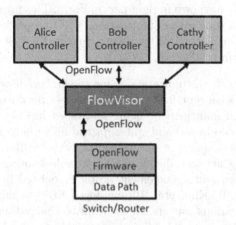

Fig. 1. Overview of FlowVisor scheme

Slices can be defined by any combination of switch ports (layer 1), source and destination Ethernet addresses or types (layer 2), source and destination IP addresses or types (layer 3), and source and destination TCP/UDP ports [8] or ICMP code/type (layer 4) [9]. It means each slice/VNO has its own flow space which is employed to distinguish traffic of different slices/VNOs.

FlowVisor enforces isolation between each slice, i.e., one slice cannot control another slice's traffic. Every slice has its own flow controller as well as the logical view. This is control plane isolation. As for the data plane isolation, FlowVisor could leverage hardware capability and OpenFlow protocol to provide bandwidth isolation. For example, OpenFlow protocol has already exposed hardware bandwidth slicing capabilities in the form of per-port queues. Thus, the traffic isolation could be guaranteed through queue scheduling, which means different queues could be designated to different slices/VNOs.

However, the FlowVisor solution has several drawbacks:

1. Since no specific mechanism/messages in OpenFlow protocol (latest 1.5 version) could help controller and switch to communicate queue-related information, e.g. queue scheduling algorithm, queue number, queue priority, queue affiliation, guaranteed/ceiling rate, and so on. Thus, FlowVisor could not obtain detailed queue information of underlying devices.

Consequently, FlowVisor has no knowledge of deciding which queue the flow/packet should be put into, let alone QoS assurance.

2. Generally, each slice/VNO could define its own Openflow table item, as shown in the left part of Fig. 3. But, basically VNOs have no knowledge of queue configuration, which is usually dominated by infrastructure operator. For the purpose of shielding or security, it is better not exposing queue details to VNOs. Thus, the VNO controller could not decide which queue the flow/-packet should be put into. It is necessary for the FlowVisor to inject queue value in each flow table item, which eventually would be delivered to the underlying switch, as shown in right part of Fig. 3. This injection action should be performed based on queue information, VNO property and even the flow characteristics. Currently, in FlowVisor solution, there is no specific module that could perform this action.

In terms of network customization, some researchers have made some trials on introducing SDN concept into traditional access networks. The three main problems in network management being addressed include: enabling frequent changes to network conditions and states, providing support for network configurations in a high-level language, and providing better visibility and control over tasks for performing network diagnosis and troubleshooting. To deal with the network configuration and management problems existed in the current state-of-the-art networks, H. Kim. etc. [10] employed SDN to improve the network management from various aspects. In addition to the systems themselves, various prototype deployments [11–14] have demonstrated how SDN can improve common network management tasks and enable business applications in campus and carrier networks.

Network slicing also has been discussed a lot in access network especially in the PON systems [14–19]. The major research activities focus on the physical or cross-layer protocol design for multiple concurrent network applications, e.g. 5G X-hauling, IoT services, and low-latency applications, etc.

In order to address the drawbacks of the existing work, we propose a novel OpenFlow-extended queue scheduling for multi-tenants in the access network.

3   Motivation and Problem Statement

Network operators are facing a very challenging problem, that is, the growth rate of revenue is far behind the growth rate of data traffic and cost. These differences in these growth rates lead to a significant income gap. In order to narrow the revenue gap and achieve a sustainable business model, one effective approach is to increase the revenue per bit through specialized network framework and customized service provision. In the highly competitive telecommunications industry, in order to create differentiation, network operators are willing to implement their own optimized protocols and provide subscribers with more and more customization possibilities. This appeal urges operators to abstract underlying network infrastructure and provides standard application programming interfaces at different levels. The concept of SDN, which separates the control plane

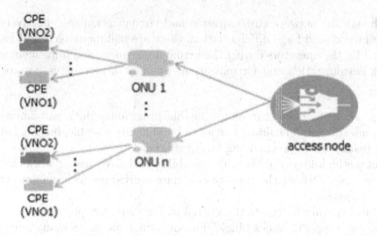

Fig. 2. Access network slicing

Table ID	Table item
0	Match{....}, action {Goto 100}
100	Match{ds=10.67.121.0, tcp_port=554}, action {output: 2}
...	...
300	Match{eth_type=arp}, action {drop}

Flow table in VNO controller

Table ID	Table item
0	Match{....}, action {Goto 100}
100	Match{ds=10.67.121.0, tcp_port=554}, action {output: 2, set_queue: 3}
...	...
300	Match{eth_type=arp}, action {drop}

Flow table in switch

Fig. 3. Queue value injection

from the data plane, just meets this requirement exactly. Moving most of the complexity of physical devices to a centralized computing pool allows easier management of those functions, and efficiently supports customized requirements in a software-defined way. Consequently, the telecommunication network can easily be programmed or reprogrammed in an IT manner in real-time. Operators can conveniently customize their environments to enable rapid service innovation.

Another approach to narrow the revenue gap is to resort to network virtualization and network slicing, which could lower the cost per bit. Network virtualization provides a powerful way to run multiple networks, each of which is customized to a specific purpose, at the same time over a shared substrate. With the benefit of network virtualization, network provider owns a physical access network that could support multi-tenancy, where network provider's access network may be used by other service providers or network tenants. In this way, the access network, as a highly multiplexed shared environment, could simultaneously offers multiple different tenants with on-demand use of network resources that may have different network characteristics. Each tenant would have its own dedicated network instance which provides complete functions just like a physical network element. Many virtual access node (VAN) instances with fully functionalities implemented on physical access node will be provided to different tenants.

Although the network customization and virtualization can effectively drive revenue growth and forge differentiation, there are still many technical issues to be solved for the operators during the actual deployment and implementation of network customization and virtualization. The key intractable issues are listed as below.

– What kind of architecture could enable programmability, automation and customization, and facilitate carrier to build highly scalable, flexible networks that readily adapt to changing business needs?
– What methodology could provide the ability to deliver new network capability and services without the need to configure individual devices or waiting for vendor releases?
– How to dynamically create the virtual instances on the physical device while providing support for flexibility? Through what means to manage/control/-maintain these virtual instances while reducing the OPEX?
– How to support customized requirements of multi-tenants? For example, how to make one MDU (Multiple Dwelling Unit) serve for multi-tenants simultaneously; How to provide flexible baseband protocol and configurable packet processing to different tenants?
– How to support different access technologies (e.g. ADSL, G.fast, EPON) simultaneously without dedicated processing board (line termination board)? For example, one virtual access node may support ADSL protocol at one moment, and support G.fast protocol (even EPON) at another moment.
– How to support dynamic port/link configuration for various deployment scenarios? How to dynamically change the serving object of one physical port on MDU or OLT (Optical Line Terminal)? It implies that one MDU/OLT physical port may serve for one VNO (Virtual Network Operator) at one moment, and serve for other VNOs at another moment.

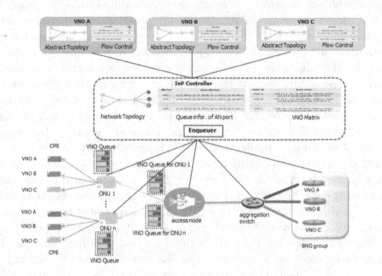

Fig. 4. Architecture of access network sharing

These emerging problems push the industry to explore new methodologies to allow enterprises and carriers to gain unprecedented programmability, automation, and network control, and enable them to build highly scalable and flexible networks that readily adapt to changing business needs. Software defined networking, decoupling the control plane and data plane of the network, has been considered as a potential solution, which can meet all these challenges. From the perspective of access network, SDN concept could offer a more intelligent and automatic network framework, which facilitates fast service provisioning and enables a wide variety of access technologies. Based on these observations, this paper aims to design a new SDN-based architecture for fixed access network, which can provide cost-efficient network control and management with high scalability and customization support.

4   Basic Idea of the Solution

In order to support multi-tenants sharing the same fixed access network, especially the access node and ONU, we extend OpenFlow protocol and introduce a queue scheduling methodology for traffic isolation and QoS guarantee. The whole architecture is shown in Fig. 4.

The main contributions of this paper can be summarized as below.

1. We introduce a queue scheduling mechanism for multi-tenants. According to the hardware capability, the queue scheduling could be implemented on Access Node or ONU. Option 1: the Access Node maintains a queue set (composed of several queues) for each ONU; In the queue set, different queues would be designated to different VNOs. Note that multiple queues could serve for one VNO. Option 2: ONU maintains only one queue set for different VNOs. In the queue set, different queues would be designated to different VNOs. The difference from option 1 is that there no specific queue set for each CPE.
2. We introduce a new module "Enqueuer" into InP controller (Infrastructure Provider controller), which is responsible for adding the queue action into flow table item. When VNOs deliver specific flow table item (mainly those configured with detailed output port) to InP controller, the "Enqueuer" module designates the queue value in the action field according to the queue information, VNO matrix and flow property. Then, the "Enqueuer" module injects the queue value in the original flow table item and delivers it to underlying devices (in our case, ONU or Access Node).
3. New data structs and property fields are defined and introduced into OpenFlow protocol to indicate queue-related information. Through these extensions, the controller would have the capability to get queue information of each port, e.g. queue number, queue scheduler, queue priority, queue affiliation, guaranteed/ceiling rate, etc. Then controller could make queue decision for each flow.

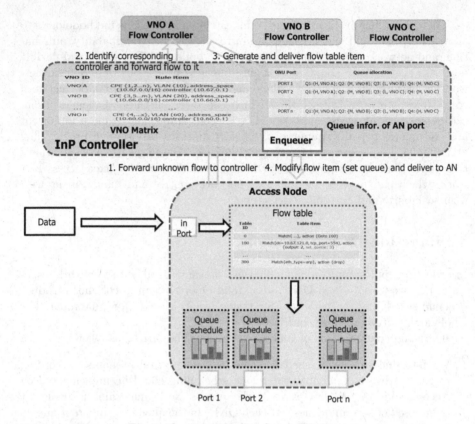

Fig. 5. Queue scheduling for multi-tenants

5   Solution Design and Implementation

This section presents the design and implementation of our approach, introducing how to slice fixed access network based on OpenFlow-enabled queue scheduling.

5.1   Solution Design and Implementation

As mentioned before, Access Node or ONU maintains several queues for different tenants/VNOs. Dedicated queue (or multi-queues) is reserved for specific tenant/VNO. According to the flow table item (with configured queue field) delivered by InP controller, Access Node or ONU could identify different traffics and set them to proper queue. It means that a slice of Access Node or ONU is created for each VNO, which could work as a fully functional Access Node or ONU with complete physical resources (port, link) and logical resources (VLAN space and other label resources). It provides fully functional access network slices for different VNOs while guaranteeing strong isolation between them.

```
enum ofp_queue_desc_prop_type {
        OFPQDPT_MIN_RATE          =0;                    /* Minimum data rate guaranteed. */
        OFPQDPT_MAX_RATE          =1;                    /* Maximum data rate. */
        OFPQDPT_PRIORITY          =2;                    /* Queue priority in SP algorithms. */
        OFPQDPT_WEIGHT            =3;                    /* Weight value in WRR algorithms. */
        OFPQDPT_AFFILIATION       =4;                    /* Queue affiliation. */
        OFPQDPT_EXPERIMENTER      =0xFFFF;               /* Experimenter defined property. */
};
/* Common header for all queue properties. */
struct ofp_queue_desc_prop_header {
        uint16_t        type;                   /* One of OFPQDPT_*. */
        uint16_t        length;                 /* Length in bytes of this property. */
}
/* queue description.*/
struct ofp_queue_desc {
        uint32_t        port_no;                        /* Port this queue is attached to. */
        uint32_t        queue_id;                       /* id for the specific queue. */
        uint16_t        len;                            /* Length in bytes of this queue desc. */
        uint8_t         pad[6];                         /* 64-bit alignment. */
        struct ofp_queue_desc_prop_header   properties [0];       /*List of properties. */
}
```

Fig. 6. Queue property type and queue description struct-1

InP controller maintains the VNO matrix, which is composed of a series of rules. Each rule item describes the properties of one VNO, such as VNO type, VNO priority, CPE identities, flow space, VNO controller IP, etc. When an unknown flow arrives at the Access Node, it would be forwarded to InP controller. According to the VNO matrix, InP controller identifies the flow and forwards it to the corresponding VNO controller. Then, the VNO controller generates and delivers flow table item to InP controller. Since the VNO controller could obtain the queue information of underlying devices (AN or ONU) through the extended OpenFlow protocol, it could decide which queue is used for forwarding the flow. The "Enqueuer" module injects proper queue value in the action field of flow table item and delivers it to the Access Node or ONU. The whole procedure is shown in Fig. 5.

In order to communicate the queue information between the controller and underlying devices, we introduce a new enum value (as shown in Fig. 6) to describe different types of queue properties, which could be included in queue description struct (ofp_queue_desc) defined in OpenFlow protocol. As shown in Fig. 7, three new property objects (ofp_queue_desc_prop_priority, ofp_queue_desc_prop_weight, ofp_queue_desc_prop_affiliation) are introduced to describe the priority, weight and affiliation property, respectively. Note that all these properties are not mandatory and they are defined and used only when applicable. For example, only when weighted round-robin algorithms are employed for queue scheduling, the weight property would be used to describe the queue weights. Only when the queue is

```
/* queue priority description.*/
struct ofp_queue_desc_prop_priority {
        uint16_t        type;              /* OFPQDPT_PRIORITY. */
        uint16_t        length;            /* Length is 8. */
        uint16_t        priority;          /* priority value. */
        uint8_t         pad[2];            /* 64-bit alignment */
}


/* queue weight description.*/
struct ofp_queue_desc_prop_weight {
        uint16_t        type;              /* OFPQDPT_WEIGHT. */
        uint16_t        length;            /* Length is 8. */
        uint16_t        weight;            /* weight value. */
        uint8_t         pad[2];            /* 64-bit alignment */
}


/* queue affilation description.*/
struct ofp_queue_desc_prop_affilation{
        uint16_t        type;              /* OFPQDPT_AFFILIATION. */.
        uint16_t        length;            /* Length is 8. */
        uint16_t        affilation;        /* Tenant ID to indicate queue affiliation.  Set 0xFF if not exclusive */
        uint8_t         pad[2];            /* 64-bit alignment */
}
```

Fig. 7. Queue property type and queue description struct-2

dedicated to one specific VNO, the affiliation property would be set to the corresponding VNO ID.

A series of queue scheduler structs are defined to describe different scheduling algorithms. As shown in Fig. 8 and Fig. 9, specific parameters are defined for different schedulers. Different queue schedulers are defined to describe different queue scheduler algorithms. Each queue scheduler struct could include multiple ofp_queue_desc structs, which describe queues under the scheduling of this queue scheduler.

As show in Fig. 10, specific queue scheduler struct would be added to ofp_port_desc_prop_* struct if the corresponding scheduling algorithm is employed on this port.

Through these extensions to OpenFlow protocol, the queue status and scheduler information could be communicated between the controller and underlying devices. Based on this information, the "Enqueuer" module can accurately make decisions and designate proper queue value in the flow action field.

Overall, this paper proposed an OpenFlow-enabled queue scheduling methodology to support multi-tenants sharing the same fixed access network. It provides fully functional access network slices for different VNOs while guaranteeing strong isolation between them. Besides, the OpenFlow protocol is extended to enable communicating the queue-relevant information between the controller and underlying devices.

```
/* HTB struct. */
struct ofp_queue_scheduler_HTB {
        uint16_t                     type;                          /* OFPQST_HTB */
        uint16_t                     length;                        /* Length in bytes of this scheduler. */
        uint16_t                     leaf_number;                   /* total leaves number. */
        uint32_t                     guaranteed_rate;               /* total guaranteed rate. */
        uint32_t                     ceil_rate;                     /* total ceiling rate. */
        struct ofp_queue_desc        queue[leaf_number];            /* property description of each queue. */
};


/* WRR struct. */
struct ofp_queue_scheduler_WRR {
        uint16_t                     type;                          /* OFPQST_WRR */
        uint16_t                     length;                        /* Length in bytes of this scheduler. */
        uint16_t                     queue_number;                  /* total queue number. */
        uint32_t                     max_weight ;                   /* maximum weight value. */
        uint32_t                     mini_weight;                   /* minimal granularity of weight. */
    struct  ofp_queue_desc           queue[queue_number];           /* property description of each queue. */
};
```

Fig. 8. New structs of queue scheduler-1

```
/* SP struct. */
struct ofp_queue_scheduler_SP {
        uint16_t                     type;                          /* OFPQST_SP */
        uint16_t                     length;                        /* Length in bytes of this scheduler. */
        uint16_t                     queue_number;                  /* total queue number. */
        uint32_t                     highest_priority;              /* value of the highest priority . */
        uint32_t                     lowest_priority;               /* value of the lowest priority. */
        struct ofp_queue_desc        queue[queue_number];           /* property description of each queue. */
};

/* no queue description defined in FIFO struct . */
struct ofp_queue_scheduler_FIFO {
        uint16_t                     type;                          /* OFPQST_FIFO*/
        uint16_t                     length;                        /* Length in bytes of this scheduler. */
};

/* queue scheduler types */
enum ofp_queue_scheduler_type {
        OFPQST_HTB         =0;                  /* HTB scheduler. */
        OFPQST_WRR         =1;                  /* WRR scheduler. */
        OFPQST_SP          =2;                  /* SP scheduler. */
        OFPQST_FIFO        =3;                  /* FIFO scheduler. */
        OFPQST_EXPERIMENTER    =0xFFFF;         /* Experimenter scheduler. */
};
```

Fig. 9. New structs of queue scheduler-2

```
/* Ethernet port description property. */
   struct ofp_port_desc_prop_ethernet {
      uint16_t    type;                                    /* OFPPDPT_ETHERNET. */
      uint16_t    length;                                  /* Length in bytes of this property. */
      uint8_t     pad[4];                                  /* Align to 64 bits. */
   /* Bitmaps of OFPPF_* that describe features. All bits zeroed if
   unsupported or unavailable. */
      uint32_t    curr;                                    /* Current features. */
      uint32_t    advertised;                              /* Features being advertised by the port. */
      uint32_t    supported;                               /* Features supported by the port. */
      uint32_t    peer;                                    /* Features advertised by peer. */
      uint32_t    curr_speed;                              /* Current port bitrate in kbps. */
      uint32_t    max_speed;                               /* Max port bitrate in kbps */
      uint16_t    max_queue ;                              /* Max amount of queue; zero if unsupported */
      struct ofp_queue_scheduler_header  scheduler;       /* dedicated scheduler property*/
   };
```

Fig. 10. Extension to port property description struct

6   Conclusion

The rise of 5g technology greatly promotes the development of communication network, and a large number of new business scenarios emerge, such as network slicing, and so on. In order to support multi-tenants sharing the same fixed access network, especially the access node and ONU, in this paper we propose a novel queue scheduling mechanism for multi-tenants by extending OpenFlow protocol and introduce a queue scheduling methodology for traffic isolation and QoS guarantee. Besides, a new "Enqueuer" module is introduced for the SDN controller to perform centralized queue management and guarantee strong isolation between different VNOs.

References

1. Openflow swtich specifications. https://www.opennetworking.org/sdn-resources/onf-specifications. OPEN NETWORKING FOUNDATION
2. McKeown, N., et al.: OpenFlow: enabling innovation in campus networks. ACM SIGCOMM comput. Commun. Rev. **38**(2), 69–74 (2008)
3. Open networking foundation. https://www.opennetworking.org
4. Kerpez, K., Cioffi, J., Ginis, G., Goldburg, M., Galli, S., Silverman, P.: Software-defined access networks. IEEE Commun. Mag. **52**(9), 152–159 (2014)
5. Hu, F., Hao, Q., Bao, K.: A survey on software-defined network and OpenFlow: from concept to implementation. IEEE Commun. Surv. Tutor. **16**(4), 2181–2206 (2014)
6. Sherwood, R., et al.: FlowVisor: a network virtualization layer. OpenFlow Switch Consortium, Technical report, vol. 1, p. 132 (2009)
7. Oktian, Y.E., Lee, S., Lee, H., Lam, J.: Distributed SDN controller system: a survey on design choice. Comput. Netw. **121**, 100–111 (2017)

8. Forouzan, B.A.: TCP/IP Protocol Suite. McGraw-Hill Higher Education (2002)
9. Li, X., Bao, C., Baker, F.: IP/ICMP translation algorithm. Internet Engineering Task Force, RFC, vol. 6145 (2011)
10. Kim, H., Feamster, N.: Improving network management with software defined networking. IEEE Commun. Mag. **51**(2), 114–119 (2013)
11. Alvarez, P., Slyne, F., Blumm, C., Marquezbarja, J., Dasilva, L., Ruffini, M.: Experimental demonstration of SDN-controlled variable-rate fronthaul for converged LTE-over-PON. In: Optical Fiber Communication Conference (2018)
12. Kosmetos, E., Matrakidis, C., Stevdas, A., Orfanoudakis, T.: An SDN architecture for PON networks enabling unified management using abstractions. In: 2018 European Conference on Optical Communication (ECOC), pp. 1–3 (2018)
13. Parol, P., Pawlowski, M.: Towards networks of the future: SDN paradigm introduction to PON networking for business applications. In: 2013 Federated Conference on Computer Science and Information Systems, pp. 829–836 (2013)
14. Hwang, I.-S., Tesi, C., Pakpahan, A.F., Ab-Rahman, M.S., Liem, A.T., Rianto, A.: Software-defined time-shifted IPTV architecture for locality-awareness TWDM-PON. Optik **207**, 164179 (2020)
15. Schneir, J.R., Xiong, Y.: Cost analysis of network sharing in FTTH/PONs. IEEE Commun. Mag. **52**(8), 126–134 (2014)
16. Uzawa, H., Honda, K., Nakamura, H., Hirano, Y., Terada, J.: Dynamic bandwidth allocation scheme for network-slicing-based TDM-PON toward the beyond-5G era. J. Opt. Commun. Netw. **12**(2), A135-143 (2019)
17. Dong, L., Gu, R., Guo, Q., Ji, Y.: Demonstration of multi-vendor multi-standard PON networks for network slicing in 5G-oriented mobile network. In: Asia Communications and Photonics Conference (2017)
18. Gu, R., Zhang, S., Ji, Y., Yan, Z.: Network slicing and efficient ONU migration for reliable communications in converged vehicular and fixed access network. Veh. Commun. S2214209617301584 (2018)
19. Zhang, L., et al.: Service-aware network slicing supporting delay-sensitive services for 5G fronthaul. In: 2018 Proceedings Paper (2018)

Research and Improvement on Detection Algorithm of SCMA System

Chenglin Liu[✉], Yanyong Su, Ruiran Liu, and Zhongshuai Qin

Harbin Institute of Technology, Harbin, China
1625830074@qq.com

Abstract. In this paper, a grouping low-complexity MPA detection algorithm (DPG-MPA) based on dynamic pruning is proposed to solve the problem of high computational complexity at the receiver of SCMA system. In this algorithm, users are grouped into groups, and the user nodes in the group adopt the serial message transmission mode, and the priority of updating user information is judged according to the node convergence degree of user information. After a predetermined number of iterations, residual values of user nodes are calculated, nodes whose residual values are lower than the threshold value are marked as trusted nodes, and information values on trusted nodes are stopped in subsequent iterations. Simulation results show that the proposed algorithm can accelerate convergence and reduce redundant operations without losing the system's excellent bit error performance.

Keywords: SCMA · MPA · Algorithm

1 The Introduction

5G and satellite Iot systems connect everything through information processing and transmission technology, which supports a large number of users and fierce competition for spectrum resources. Multiple access technology has an important impact on the overall capacity and access capacity of the system. Sparse Code Multiple Access (SCMA) technology can realize overload transmission. However, with the increase of overload, the interference between codes and words increases, and the system error performance deteriorates, and the decoding complexity is very high. Therefore, it is worth studying to reduce the decoding complexity of high order systems on the premise of good error performance. In this paper, a new DPG-MPA algorithm is proposed to reduce the decoding complexity of SCMA system effectively.

2 Research on Principle and Decoding Algorithm of Serial SCMA System

2.1 System Description

Figure 1 shows the block diagram of the codec scheme of the serial SCMA system, which contains the first-level SCMA coding module at the transmitting end and $P - 1$

© ICST Institute for Computer Sciences, Social Informatics and Telecommunications Engineering 2022
Published by Springer Nature Switzerland AG 2022. All Rights Reserved
K. Wu et al. (Eds.): ICECI 2021, LNICST 437, pp. 74–79, 2022.
https://doi.org/10.1007/978-3-031-04231-7_6

Pattern matrix module $\mathbf{G}_p$, where c The whole transmitting module is divided into P sub-modules. In the serial encoding SCHEME of SCMA system, user binary bits are first mapped to low order SCMA(K_1, N_1, M_1) complex field code words by the first level SCMA system. Then it is processed by the P – 1 order $\mathbf{G}_p$ serial subsystem. The system overload is increased step by step, and finally the coding words of high order SCMA system are obtained.

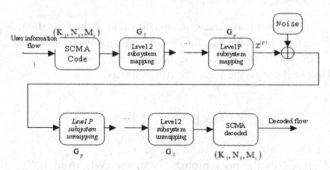

Fig. 1. Block diagram of codec scheme of serial SCMA system

2.2 Algorithm Research and Design

SCMA code words are sparse, the MPA algorithm originally used in LDPC decoder can be used for multi-user detection. However, with the expansion of the system scale, the complexity of MPA algorithm is still too high, resulting in high requirements on hardware, which is impossible to implement in reality. Therefore, it is necessary to further study how to reduce the computational complexity of MPA algorithm. The process of traditional MPA algorithm is as follows.

Step 1: initialize the prior probabilities of all code words for each user and the function information at the resource node.

Assuming that the code word sent by the user is prior and equal, the information at the user node is initialized as:

$$I^0_{v_j \to g_k}(x_j) = \frac{1}{M}, \forall j \tag{1}$$

The conditional probability is calculated at the resource node

$$\phi_k = \exp\left(-\frac{1}{2\sigma^2}\left\|y_k - \sum_{m \in \xi_k} h_{k,m} x_{k,m}\right\|^2\right) \tag{2}$$

Where $I^t_{g_k \to v_j}(x_j)$ represents the message update value of the t round iteration, $h_{k,m}$ and $x_{k,m}$ represent the channel coefficient and codebook component of user M transmitted on subcarrier K.

Step 2: Iterate message passing based on factor graph to update message values from RN to UN.

$$I_{g_k \to v_j}^t (x_j) = \sum_{\sim x_j} \left\{ \frac{1}{\sqrt{2\pi}\sigma} \exp\left(-\frac{1}{2\sigma^2} \left\| y_k - \sum_{m \in \xi_k} h_{k,m} x_{k,m} \right\|^2 \right) \times \prod_{l \in \xi_k / \{j\}} I_{v_l \to g_k}^{t-1} (x_l) \right\}$$

(3)

where, $I_{g_k \to v_j}^t (x_j)$ represents the message update value in the t iteration, $h_{k,m}$ and $x_{k,m}$ represent the channel coefficient and codeword component of user M transmitted on subcarrier K respectively. $\xi_k / \{j\}$ is all the elements in ξ_k minus j.

Step 3: Update the message values from UN to RN.

$$I_{v_j \to g_k}^t (x_j) = N \left(\Pr(x_j) \prod_{m \in \zeta_j / \{k\}} I_{g_m \to v_j}^t (x_j) \right)$$

(4)

where $\Pr(x_j)$ represents the prior probability of the code word x_j. $N(\cdot)$ represents a normalized function.

Step 4: Output the decoding result. When the number of iterations reaches the target number of iterations T, the decision is made. Calculate the probability value of each code word:

$$Q(x_j) = \prod_{k \in \zeta_j} I_{g_k \to v_j}^T (x_j), \forall j$$

(5)

The maximum value of $Q(x_j)$ corresponds to the code word information and the detected code word information of user J.

The S-MPA scheme takes advantage of the principle that new messages obtained when updating a single node can be immediately used for message updating of other nodes in the same iteration, thus sequential updating of UN messages during the same iteration. For $1 \le j \le J$ and $k \in \zeta_j$, the message update processes for RN and UN are processed jointly. Message update processes for RN and UN are processed jointly. The convergence process can be accelerated by using more reliable messages during iteration, and Formula (3) is modified as

$$I_{g_k \to v_j}^t (x_j)$$
$$= \sum_{\sim x_j} \left\{ \frac{1}{\sqrt{2\pi}\sigma} \exp\left(-\frac{1}{2\sigma^2} \left\| y_k - \sum_{m \in \xi_k} h_{k,m} x_{k,m} \right\|^2 \right) \times \prod_{\substack{l \in \xi_k / \{j\} \\ l<j}} I_{v_l \to g_k}^t (x_l) \prod_{\substack{l \in \xi_k / \{j\} \\ l>j}} I_{v_l \to g_k}^{t-1} (x_l) \right\}$$

(6)

PM-MPA algorithm introduces two user parameters M and R_s, based on these two parameters to control the algorithm complexity. The current number of cycles is t, the total number of cycles is t. At that time, the resource node fed back information to the user node according to the original MPA algorithm. When $t = m$, select $i = R_s/d_c$

element in $\hat{\mathbf{x}}^m$. $\hat{\mathbf{x}}^m$ represents the estimator of user node information $\hat{\mathbf{x}}$ obtained after the mth iteration. The PM-MPA algorithm selects the last i elements, $\hat{\mathbf{x}}^m$ are divided into two parts. When $t > m$, the last i elements $\bar{\mathbf{x}}$ are used in place of x, and the information of the first node in x is updated during the subsequent loop. And updates the information of the previous $J - i$ node in x during the subsequent loop.

Max-log-MPA introduce MPA algorithm into logarithmic domain and use maximum approximation, the original large number of exponential operations and multiplication operations are simplified into simple operations such as summation and comparison. Use the following relationship:

$$\log\left(\sum_{i=1}^{N}\exp(f_i)\right) \approx \max_{i=1,...,N}\{f_1, f_2, ..., f_N\} \tag{7}$$

By applying the above formula to MPA detection algorithm and combining with Formula (3), the original formula can be simplified as

$$L_{g_k \to v_j}^t(x_j) \doteq \max\left(-\frac{1}{2\sigma^2}\left\|y_k - \sum_{m\in\xi_k} h_{k,m}x_{k,m}\right\|^2\right) + \sum_{l\in\xi_k/\{j\}} L_{v_l \to g_k}^{t-1}(x_l) \tag{8}$$

Combining formula (7) and Formula (4), it can be obtained:

$$L_{v_j \to g_k}^t(x_j) = \sum_{m\in\zeta_j/\{k\}} L_{g_m \to v_j}^{t-1}(x_j) + \Pr(x_j) \tag{9}$$

The algorithm proposed in this paper comprehensively utilizes the advantages of the above three improved schemes, proposes a grouping of low-complexity MPA (DPG-MPA) based on dynamic pruning, and further optimizes the performance of MPA algorithm. The process is as follows:

Step 1: Input known information, including user codebook, factor graph matrix, noise and channel parameters, signal y received by decoding end, number of user groups G, total number of iterations T, number of pruning start iteration T1, node residual value threshold TH, etc.

Step 2: initialize the user node information according to Formula (1). The update sequence set of user nodes is seted as $\Phi(t)$, initialized as $\Phi(1) = \{1, 2, ..., J\}$, and update the user node information in the original order. After each iteration, the user subscript order in $\Phi(t)$ will be updated according to the convergence degree of user nodes.

Step 3: Start iterating when t < T. Starting from the user node corresponding to the subscript of the first element in set $\Phi(t)$, determine which group this user node belongs to, calculate the updated message $L_{g_k \to v_j}^t(x_j)$ at this user node according to Formula (8), and jointly update $L_{v_j \to g_k}^t(x_j)$ according to formula (9).

All the edge residuals $R_{v_j \to g_k}^t$ were calculated according to the factor graph, and the convergence degree M_j was reached according to the edge residuals. Set $\Phi(t)$ was updated as $\Phi(t + 1)$ for the next iteration.

If $t < T_1$, $t = t + 1$. if $t \geq T_1$, Then compute the node residuals R_j^t of all user nodes that are not marked as trusted nodes. Mark the user node $R_j^t <$ th as a trusted node. And delete the subscript of this node in $\Phi(t + 1)$, Then, $T = T + 1$.

Step 4: End the iteration and obtain the decoding result according to Formula (5).

2.3 Performance Analysis of Decoding Algorithm

Figure 2 shows the calculation amount of MPA, PM-mpa, S-MPA and DPG-MPA algorithms in addition, multiplication and exponential operation in an SCMA system with 6 users and 4 resource nodes. In the PM-MPA algorithm $m = 3$, $R_s = 2$ In the DPG-MPA algorithm, $T_1 = 1$, th $= 10^{-6}$.

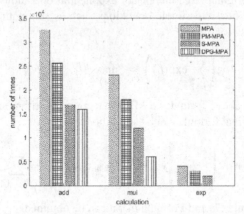

Fig. 2. Comparison of computation amount between different decoding algorithms

It can be seen from Fig. 2 that compared with MPA algorithm, DPG-MPA algorithm can reduce the amount of computation by about 50%, and the degree of reduction varies according to the threshold value, the number of initial iterations of pruning operation and other parameters.

Figure 3 shows the ber curves of MPA algorithm, S-MPA algorithm and DPG-MPA algorithm under different iterations. The SCMA system adopted has 6 users, 4 resource nodes, 150% overload and SNR $= 6$. In the PM-MPA algorithm $m = 3$, $R_s = 2$ In the DPG-MPA algorithm, $T_1 = 1$, th $= 10^{-6}$.

According to Fig. 3, when the number of iterations is large enough, the ber of each algorithm tends to converge. Both S-MPA algorithm and DPG-MPA algorithm can accelerate the convergence process, thus achieving lower computational complexity. In addition, the bit error rate of DPG-MPA algorithm is lower than that of S-MPA algorithm in the first three iterations, indicating that DPG-MPA algorithm has better convergence performance.

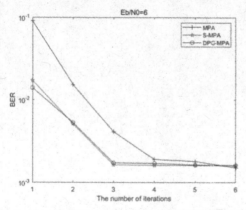

Fig. 3. SER performance curve of different decoding algorithms changing with the number of iterations

3 Conclusion

All the decoding algorithms studied in this paper are based on the improvement of MPA algorithm. The DPG-MPA algorithm proposed in this paper can further reduce the complexity of the decoding algorithm while ensuring less loss of the system's bit error performance.

At the same time, the decoding research work in this paper is based on the ideal condition of complete synchronization of signals at the receiving end, and the synchronization deviation of signals will greatly affect the performance of the decoding end. How to minimize synchronization deviation has important research value and can be further studied.

References

1. Klimentyev, V.P., Sergienko, A.B.: SCMA codebooks optimization based on genetic algorithm. In: 23th European Wireless Conference on European Wireless 2017, pp. 1–6 (2017)
2. Mu, H., Ma, Z., Alhaji, M., et al.: A fixed low complexity message pass algorithm detector for up-link SCMA system. IEEE Wirel. Commun. Lett. **4**(6), 585–588 (2015)
3. Yang, L., Liu, Y., Siu, Y.: Low complexity message passing algorithm for SCMA system. IEEE Commun. Lett. **20**(12), 2466–2469 (2016)
4. Aji, S.M., McEliece, R.J.: A general algorithm for distributing information in a graph. In: Proceedings of IEEE International Symposium on Information Theory, p. 6 (1997)

Internet of Things

A Survey of Adversarial Attacks on Wireless Communications

Xiangyu Luo[1], Quan Qin[1], Xueluan Gong[2(✉)], and Meng Xue[2(✉)]

[1] School of Cyber Science and Engineering, Wuhan University, Wuhan, China
{ericlaw,2019302180109}@whu.edu.cn
[2] School of Computer Science, Wuhan University, Wuhan, China
{xueluangong,xuemeng}@whu.edu.cn

Abstract. As the deep neural network (DNN) has been applied in various fields in wireless communications, the potential security problems of DNNs in wireless applications have not been fully studied yet. In particular, DNNs are highly vulnerable to malicious disturbance, which opens up opportunities for a small scale of adversarial attacks to cause chaos in the model's performance. This paper enumerates the main over-the-air attack mechanisms that threaten a wide range of existing defenses. For each type of attack, we introduce the working principle and list some of the latest applications in different wireless communication fields. With the threats of various attacks to a wide range of existing defenses shown, we hope to raise awareness of the lack of novel defense mechanisms.

Keywords: Wireless communication · Adversarial attack · Deep neural network · Machine learning

1 Introduction

In recent years, Deep Learning (DL) has greatly benefited from advances in computational resources and algorithmic designs, which can be leveraged to help with data processing and complicated calculating tasks. On account of underlying channels, potential interference, traffic effects, and interactions of network protocol, DL has been applied to wireless systems in various sub-fields. For instance, spectrum sensing, interference management, waveform design, and signal classification [1].

However, adversaries are able to tamper with the model by manipulating the input, algorithm, and training process of Machine Learning. Although expressly, it is acknowledged that Deep Neural Networks (DNNs) are highly vulnerable to malicious disturbance, a small-scale adversarial attack may cause chaos in the performance of the model [2], as first mentioned in the computer vision field [3]. Moreover, due to the nature of broadcast and sharing of wireless communications, the model of which is more likely to be perturbed. Thus, we will be capable of guarding against most adversaries by making safety adoption with full knowledge of the attack methods.

In this paper, we discuss five primary wireless attacks. We introduce the working principle of each type of wireless attack and list some of the latest applications in different

K. Wu et al. (Eds.): ICECI 2021, LNICST 437, pp. 83–91, 2022.
https://doi.org/10.1007/978-3-031-04231-7_7

sub-fields of wireless communication. The main principle and features of each type of over-the-air attack are listed in Table 1.

Table 1. Different types of over-the-air attacks and the features

Attack type	Principle	Attack mechanism	Attacker's access	Innovation
Evasion attacks	Perturb an ML model at inference time	Targeted evasion attack	White-box	Masquerade as a specific signal
		Untargeted evasion attack	Black-box	Low power requirement
		Physical evasion attack	Black-box	More destructive, on autoencoder system
Poisoning attacks	Pollute the training dataset	LEB attack	Black-box	Effective on fusion center, generic
		Over-the-air spectrum data poisoning attack	Black-box	Fast, hard to detect
Trojan attacks	Insert Trojans to training data	Wireless signal classification Trojan attack	All	Modify few data, practical, work on wireless signal classifier
		BadNet	All	Powerful, generic
Spoofing attacks	Using a GAN to generate and transmit synthetic signals	GAN-based wireless signal spoofing	Black-box	GAN-based, high success probability, no need for prior knowledge
		Replay spoofing attack	Black-box	Keep some features in original signals
Inference attacks	Steal the training data and fool the target model using the data	Over-the-air MIA	Black-box	Effective, first over-the-air MIA attack

2   Attack Mechanisms

2.1   The Evasion Attacks

The evasion attacks perturb the ML model at inference time by subtle modifications on the original data. It happens only when adversarial examples are used to feed the network. Adversarial examples are carefully perturbed input that looks the same as its untampered copy but with slight noise added and successfully fool the classifier of the network [4].

Current research demonstrated that DNNs are vulnerable to over-the-air adversarial evasion attacks, which significantly lower the accuracy of wireless communication tasks with only tiny modifications on the underlying transmission to a cooperative receiver [5].

Targeted Evasion Attacks
In [5], Samuel and Matthew focus on targeted evasion attacks to spectrum sensing that seek to disguise as a specific signal. They use an eavesdropper that uses a DL-based Automatic Modulation Classification (AMC) system that classifies and intercepts wireless signals when necessary. They use the RML2016.10A dataset and train the DNN model on AM-SSB. They adapt the MI-FGSM attack to RFML creating untargeted adversarial samples to compare untargeted and targeted attacks further. They find that the energy required to succeed in a targeted attack is related to the hierarchical relationship. They also draw the conclusion that the difficulty of targeting modulation schemes was confirmed.

Untargeted Evasion Attacks to Radio Signal Classification
The work presented in [6] is based on a DNN architecture using the RML2016.10A dataset. They used eavesdroppers but pre-assume that the eavesdroppers are capable of intercepting the processing chain without affecting the channel simultaneously. The authors adapt FGSM and Universal Adversarial Perturbations (UAP) to show the time-independent black-box results. They regard it as a limitation of FGSM. They also use the energy ratios of the perturbation signals as an attack limitation, just like what [4] did. Therefore, they only consider attacks with direct access to the classifier without transmitted OTA.

End-to-end Autoencoder Communication Systems
Recent research shows that end-to-end autoencoder communication systems through DNNs have a significant potential vulnerability to physical evasion attacks that result in more errors at the receiver [7]. The authors present algorithms to elaborate ways to craft effective physical black-box adversarial attacks. They finally conclude that the broadcast nature of wireless communication channels opens up great opportunities for adversary transmitters to increase the block-error rate of a communication system by well-designed perturbation signals over the channel. According to the result above, the authors put forward a possible defense assumption of adversarial training that trains the autoencoder with adversarial perturbations to increase robustness. Nevertheless, it would reduce the performance of the autoencoder and may be steered through newly designed adversarial perturbations.

2.2 The Poisoning Attacks

A poisoning attack aims to pollute the training dataset in order to produce a lousy classifier. First proposed by Barreno and Nelson [8], poisoning attacks have affected malware detection [9], collaborative filtering systems [10], face recognition [11], automatic driving [12], medical insurance [13], loan evaluation [14], and various other application scenarios.

Poison attacks are divided into two types depending on the object to poison-the data poisoning and model poisoning. Data poisoning mainly refers to combining the poison data with the original sample and feeding the polluted input to the model to generate a backdoor during the test time. Model poisoning mainly refers to offering a poisoned model to the users directly.

Over-the-Air Spectrum Sensing Data Poisoning Attacks
In recent research of spectrum data poisoning [15], the authors introduced an adversarial ML approach to complete a spectrum data poisoning attack by capturing the behavior of the transmitters and simulating the wireless spectrum sensing data. Furthermore, they propose a new type of poisoning attack based on adversarial ML called an *over-the-air spectrum data poisoning attack*. It intercepts the spectrum sensing data and seeks to manipulate it in order that wrong transmits decisions are made using unreliable spectrum sensing results.

The authors show the efficiency of such an attack since only little time is needed to manipulate the transmitter's decisions. Additionally, the short transmission makes it hard to detect such an attack. The results show that the proposed spectrum poisoning attack is more energy-efficient and more covert compared to jamming of data transmissions, which calls for awareness of new defense mechanisms in protecting wireless communications against such attacks.

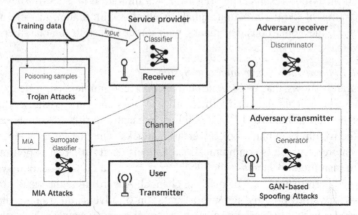

Fig. 1. Trojan attacks, MIA attacks, and GAN-based spoofing attacks in a wireless communication environment.

Learning-Empowered Poisoning Attacks
Zhengping Luo and Shangqing Zhao etc. proposed a new data poisoning mechanism in recent research [16]. They point out that a wide range of existing defense mechanisms tends to assume network or attackers as passive entities. For instance, A defender may assume that the prior attacks are known or solved. However, adversaries can

adopt arbitrary behaviors to avoid pre-assumed patterns to trounce the defense strategies. Thus, they propose a learning-empowered poisoning attack framework called Learning-Evaluation-Beating (LEB) to mislead the fusion center.

They attempt to make malicious use of ML to build a surrogate model of the fusion center's decision model, based on the black-box nature of the fusion center in spectrum data sensing. In order to create malicious sensing data, they put forward an algorithm using the surrogate model.

The results show that the LEB attacks reach a success probability of up to 82%, proving that the LEB offers an effective attack paradigm against cooperative spectrum sensing to some extent. Furthermore, the authors designed a mechanism called influence-limiting defense to couple with the LEB and other attacks with similar mechanisms.

2.3   The Trojan Attacks

Trojan attacks on wireless signal classification target DL applications [17], which use a DL classifier to classify signals (i.e., I/Q samples) with modulation types as labels, and only specific types can obtain authorization. However, unlike Trojan attacks on neural networks [18], this attack algorithm does not require access to the original model. Instead, only a small amount of manipulation of the training data is enough to implant the Trojan. And then, in the test (inference) phase, an adversary can make the model correctly classify clean input but perform not reliably on signals with Trojan triggers so that the thief can bypass the defenses and gain user authentication.

There are two periods of time to execute the attack, the training time and the test time. An adversary needs to select a label as the target label in the first step in the training time. In the second step, the adversary has to poison some non-target labeled data but simultaneously keeps the same amount of clean data for each non-target label in the training data, as presented in Fig. 1. The specific operation of poisoning is to select samples from training data randomly, rotate the samples by a specific angle θ, and finally change the non-target labels in these data to the target label. The third step is to replace the original clean samples with the poisoned samples.

The attacker uses the modulated signal from a non-target label to transmit the poisoned samples in the testing time. If the receiver classifies the received signal as the target label, the Trojan attack was successful. However, it should be noted that the value of θ can be small, so the signal-to-noise ratio does not change much, while the confidence level of the SNR estimate for small samples should be below, so the Trojan attack will not necessarily be detected by the receiver's method of checking the received SNR.

Ultimately, the Trojan attack only infects 10% of the training samples to achieve 90% attack accuracy at all SNRs. Also, for clean samples, the classification accuracy is very close to the accuracy before the implantation of the Trojan. However, this attack's changes to the training data result in outliers in the training data, so clustering-based outlier detection is effective in detecting the poisoned samples in the data and thus detecting Trojan attacks [19]. Also, according to the work of [18], the Trojan attack misleads the classifier to the same specific classification. Thus the statistics of the distribution of misclassification results should reveal that the misclassification results are mainly concentrated on one class. Therefore, another possible defense is to check the misclassification results, which will give a classification that accounts for most of the results for a Trojan attack.

2.4 The Membership Inference Attacks

A member inference attack is a type of inference attack that aims to steal training data from a target model [20]. Meanwhile, MIA for wireless signal classification allows an adversary to infer the privacy of a wireless signal, which may include wavelength, waveform, channel, and device information [21]. In an area with substantial promiscuous users, a service provider can use a classifier to classify users when performing physical layer authorization verification, and this classifier accepts signals received by the provider [22, 23]. An adversary can launch an MIA against the target classifier in this environment to confirm whether a signal belongs to the classifier's training data. Even if the adversary is in the case of a white-box attack, he cannot directly use the model available to him to determine whether a signal is from an authorized user because the signal received by the adversary will differ from the one received by the service provider. Therefore, consider directly the case of an adversary using a black-box attack, where the adversary eavesdrops on the signal and uses it as an input to a surrogate classifier built by the adversary. It is presented in Fig. 1 that the adversary can launch an MIA with this surrogate classifier to determine whether the signal received by the service provider, which corresponds to the signal eavesdropped by the adversary, is used as the training data for the target classifier.

Due to the openness of the electromagnetic environment, an adversary can collect the signals sent by the user and returned by the service provider and eavesdrop on the classification results. The adversary first needs to determine the classification of signals based on this information and build a surrogate classifier [24]. Next, the adversary uses MIA to determine whether a signal sample is used for training and if so, the signal sample leaks information about the authorized user's device, waveform Etc., which the adversary can then use to perform other attacks such as forging similar signals and gaining access.

The first of two different settings is that the signals, both member and non-member, are generated by the same device, and the second is that different devices generate the signals of non-members while the same device generates the signals of members. Eventually, the accuracy of MIA, i.e., the accuracy of predicting whether the sample is a member or a non-member, is high in the first setting, but this is when the sample signal is strong, and there is no noise. However, the accuracy of the MIA decreases significantly as soon as the sample signal weakens or noise is added. In the second setting, the accuracy of MIA and the conditions of use are generic.

The defense is mainly for the second setting on account of the low probability of success in the first setting whether exist defenses. A very effective defense method is for the service provider to create a shadow MIA and take the data to train it to get a very high attack accuracy, and then calculate the noise that can disable the shadow MIA, i.e., make this MIA much less accurate, and this noise can also be used to disable the adversary's MIA.

2.5   The Spoofing Attacks

A spoofing attack is an attacker's attempt to imitate a legitimate user in a communication. A standard method of this attack is called a replay spoofing attack [25], in which the transmission signal of a legitimate user is recorded in advance, and then the signal is replayed with the potentially altered transmission power. Although this form of attack can portray various signal characteristics, it simply records the user's transmission and is unable to imitate the combined effects formed by factors such as environment, channel, and equipment, and it also already has a detection method [26]. A better performing attack than this is the GAN-based spoofing attack [27].

GAN-based deception attacks are trained from the adversarial perspective with a generator and a discriminator, where the generator is used to generate signals that can be used in spoofing attacks, and the discriminator is used to train against the generator. Suppose that a system based on a GAN spoofing attack has four components, the transmitter T, the receiver R (a classifier that classifies the received signals as coming from T or not coming from T), the adversary transmitter AT, and the adversary receiver AR, as seen in Fig. 1. AR is located close to R so that the transmitter-to-receiver channel will be relatively similar, and AT's signal transmission will be flagged so that AR can specify which signals are sent by AT. In this case, AR acts as a discriminator to identify the signals sent by AT or T and feeds the classification result to AT. AT acts as a generator to generate signals closer to those sent by T to fool the discriminator AR. After the GAN converges, the generator AT can generate signals so similar to T that the receiver R cannot distinguish whether the signals come from AT or T, and the adversary can thus perform a spoofing attack. It can be seen that this attack does not require any prior knowledge because AR can learn the features of T by itself. Also, AR and AT will learn various channel effects during the adversarial process, and thus the attacker does not need to learn these.

GAN-based spoofing attacks' success rate is 76.2%, which is much higher than the 7.89% of random signal and 36.2% of replay spoofing attacks. The defense scheme for this type of attack needs to be further researched.

3   Conclusions

This paper enumerates five main over-the-air attack mechanisms that threaten a wide range of existing defenses. We also show some of the latest attack models and their applications, raising awareness of the lack of novel defense mechanisms. However, As the deep neural network (DNN) has been applied in various fields in wireless communications. However, the potential security problems of DNNs in wireless applications have not been fully studied yet.

References

1. Erpek, T., O'Shea, T., Sagduyu, Y., Yi Shi, T., Clancy, C.: Deep learning for wireless communications. In: Pedrycz, W., Chen, S.-M. (eds.) Development and Analysis of Deep Learning Architectures, pp. 223–266. Springer International Publishing, Cham (2020). https://doi.org/10.1007/978-3-030-31764-5_9

2. Moosavi-Dezfooli, S.-M., Fawzi, A., Fawzi, O., Frossard, P.: Universal adversarial perturbations. In: 2017 IEEE Conference on Computer Vision and Pattern Recognition, pp. 86–94 (2017)

3. Szegedy, C., Zaremba, W., Sutskever, I., Bruna, J., Erhan, D., Goodfellow, I., Fergus, R.: Intriguing properties of neural networks. arXiv preprint arXiv:1312.6199 (2013)

4. Flowers, B., Buehrer, M.R., Headley, W.C.: Evaluating Adversarial Evasion Attacks in the Context of Wireless Communications. arXiv preprint arXiv:1903.01563 (2019)

5. Bair, S., DelVecchio, M., Flowers, B., Michaels, A.J., Headley, W.C.: On the limitations of targeted adversarial evasion attacks against deep learning enabled modulation recognition. In: WiseML@WiSec, pp. 25–30 (2019)

6. Sadeghi, M., Larsson, E.G.: Adversarial attacks on deep-learning based radio signal classification. IEEE Wirel. Commun. Letters **8**, 213–216 (2018)

7. Sadeghi, M., Larsson, E.G.: Physical adversarial attacks against end-to-end autoencoder communication systems. IEEE Commun. Lett. **23**(5), 847–850 (2019)

8. Barreno, M., Nelson, B., Sears, R., et al.: Can machine learning be secure? In: The 2006 ACM Symposium on Information, Computer and Communications Security, pp. 16–25 (2006)

9. Chen, S., Xue, M.H., Fan, L.L., et al.: Automated poisoning attacks and defenses in malware detection systems: an adversarial machine learning approach. Comput. Secur. **73**, 326–344 (2018)

10. Li, B., Wang, Y., Singh, A., et al.: Data poisoning attacks on factorization-based collaborative filtering. In: Advances in Neural Information Processing Systems, pp. 1885–1893 (2016)

11. Chen, X., Liu, C., Li, B., Lu, K., et al.: Targeted backdoor attacks on deep learning systems using data poisoning. arXiv preprint arXiv:1712.05526 (2017)

12. Li, K., Mao, S.G., Li, X., et al.: Automatic lexical stress and pitch accent detection for L2 english speech using multi-distribution deep neural networks. Speech Commun. **96**, 28–36 (2018)

13. Mozaffari-Kermani, M., Sur-Kolay, S., Raghunathan, A., et al.: Systematic poisoning attacks on and defenses for machine learning in health-care. IEEE J. Biomed. Health Inform. **19**(6), 1893–1905 (2015)

14. Jagielski, M., Oprea, A., Biggio, B., et al.: Manipulating machine learning: Poisoning Attacks and countermeasures for regression learning. In: 2018 IEEE Symposium on Security and Privacy (SP), pp. 19–35 (2018)

15. Shi, Y., Erpek, T., Sagduyu, Y.E., Li, J.H.: Spectrum Data Poisoning with Adversarial Deep Learning. CoRR abs/1901.09247 (2019)

16. Luo, Z., Zhao, S., Lu, Z., Xu, J., Sagduyu, Y.E.: When Attackers Meet AI: Learning-empowered Attacks in Cooperative Spectrum Sensing. CoRR abs/1905.01430 (2019)

17. Davaslioglu, K., Sagduyu, Y.E.: Trojan attacks on wireless signal classification with adversarial machine learning. In: 2019 IEEE International Symposium on Dynamic Spectrum Access Networks (DySPAN), pp. 1–6 (2019). https://doi.org/10.1109/DySPAN.2019.8935782

18. Liu, Y., Ma, S., Safer, Y., et al.: Trojaning attack on neural networks. In: Network and Distributed System Security Symposium 2017, pp. 1–15 (2017)

19. Chen, B., et al.: Detecting backdoor attacks on deep neural networks by activation clustering. In: AAAI SafeAI (2019)

20. Shokri, R., Stronati, M., Song, C., Shmatikov, V.: Membership inference attacks against machine learning models. In: 2017 IEEE Symposium on Security and Privacy, pp. 3–18 (2017). https://doi.org/10.1109/SP.2017.41

21. Shi, Y., Sagduyu, Y.E.: Membership inference attack and defense for wireless signal classifiers with deep learning. arXiv preprint arXiv:2107.12173 (2021)

22. Wang, N., Jiang, T., Lv, S., Xiao, L.: Physical-layer authentication based on extreme learning machine. IEEE Commun. Lett. **21**(7), 1557–1560 (2017). https://doi.org/10.1109/LCOMM.2017.2690437

23. Shi, Y., Davaslioglu, K., Sagduyu, Y.E., Headley, W.C., Fowler, M., Green, G.: Deep learning for RF signal classification in unknown and dynamic spectrum environments. In: 2019 IEEE International Symposium on Dynamic Spectrum Access Networks, pp. 1–10 (2019). https://doi.org/10.1109/DySPAN.2019.8935684

24. Yi, S., Sagduyu, Y., Grushin, A.: How to steal a machine learning classifier with deep learning. In: 2017 IEEE International Symposium on Technologies for Homeland Security, pp. 1–5 (2017). https://doi.org/10.1109/THS.2017.7943475

25. Kinnunen, T., et al.: The ASVspoof 2017 Challenge: Assessing the Limits of Replay Spoofing Attack Detection (2017)

26. Hoehn, A., Zhang, P.: Detection of replay attacks in cyber-physical systems. In: 2016 American Control Conference, pp. 290–295 (2016). https://doi.org/10.1109/ACC.2016.7524930

27. Shi, Y., Davaslioglu, K., Sagduyu, Y.E.: Generative Adversarial Network for Wireless Signal Spoofing (2019)

Adversarial Examples in Wireless Networks: A Comprehensive Survey

JianShuo Dong[1], Xueluan Gong[2(✉)], and Meng Xue[2]

[1] School of Cyber Science and Engineering, Wuhan University, Wuhan, China
`jianshuo.dong@whu.edu.cn`
[2] School of Computer Science, Wuhan University, Wuhan, China
`{xueluangong,xuemeng}@whu.edu.cn`

Abstract. With the rapid development of deep learning technologies, more and more DNN models are employed in wireless communication tasks. While DNNs improve the service, they also incur potential security threats from malicious users. Adversarial Example is a generally discussed attack targeting the deep learning-based models, which undoubtedly threatens the security of deep learning-based wireless networks. In this paper, we widely investigate adversarial example attacks in wireless network scenarios. It helps us become aware of the adversarial example threats that DNNs used in wireless networks are exposed to, and more efforts are required to defend against these attacks.

Keywords: Adversarial example attacks · Wireless networks · Deep learning

1 Introduction

The progress in deep learning technologies enables deep neural networks (DNNs) to get practical applications in the real world, such as image classification and speech recognition. In wireless communities, deep neural networks are deployed to tackle various tasks like signal classification and channel management as well. While it improves efficiency and provides convenient service, it also brings more potential security risks.

Extensive researches have demonstrated that deep neural networks are vulnerable to elaborately designed adversarial perturbations. In this case, malicious attackers generate an adversarial example like a patched image or a noise-injected audio recording as input to cause incorrect output or misclassification of the victim model. Attackers can craft an adversarial example by utilizing the gradient of a model's loss function through the backward propagation algorithm.

In wireless communication scenarios, the wireless medium is shared and open to the public, meaning that the base station (BS) is more easily to be attacked by malicious users. Traditionally, attackers can jam vast queries to block the shared channel. Similarly, as discussed in [7,8,15], deep neural networks deployed in the

K. Wu et al. (Eds.): ICECI 2021, LNICST 437, pp. 92–97, 2022.
https://doi.org/10.1007/978-3-031-04231-7_8

base station are likely to suffer from practical attacks as well. So adversarial example attacks can pose a practical threat to the wireless network scenario. Through disguising the waveform, wrong signals will be transmitted to the terminal station to spoof the target DNN model. Therefore, it is meaningful for us to widely investigate adversarial attack practices in wireless networks and conclude the commonly shared features of this series of adversarial attacks.

2 Background

2.1 Adversarial Example

Adversarial example attacks mislead the target neural network by adding a specific adversarial perturbation to the input. As a consequence, the victim model may give back an unexpected output, and even worse, it may fall apart beyond expectation. As described in [1,17], this kind of attack has been widely studied and got practical success in many domains, like computer vision [3] and natural language understanding. According to attack results, AE attacks can be divided into targeted attacks and untargeted attacks. Targeted attacks aim to make the victim model misclassify adversarial examples into one specific class. In face recognition scenario, people with fabricated face disguise will be classified into a specific identity. The untargeted ones, otherwise, only seek to misguide the victim model to categorize the adversarial examples into a wrong class. As summarized in [16], to tackle adversarial example attacks, some defense strategies have been proposed. For example, network distillation [12] and adversarial train [4] technologies can be utilized to defend against adversarial example attacks.

The paper [10] points out that with more DNNs deployed in the real world, there are more practical scenarios to implement adversarial examples attacks. Under the circumstances of wireless networks, DNNs are deployed in the base station for high execution performance. However, neural networks are naturally vulnerable to attacks like AE attacks, which brings more security risks.

2.2 Wireless Network

Wireless networks provide connection services between different users within a limited geographical range. In wireless networks, signals are transmitted from node to node through wireless medium and without a physical wire connection. As described in [11], there are two typical wireless connection architectures. One is ad hoc network, in which case no central access point is involved, and each node connects directly to its neighbor nodes. Manual configuration is required to establish an ad hoc network. The other is centrally coordinated network, in which end users query the access point to obtain remote connection service. After being granted access permission, end users only send data to the access point, and the access point is in charge of transferring the data to the terminal point. In the following contents, all attacks are illustrated under the setting of centrally coordinated network.

3   Adversarial Example Attacks in Wireless Networks

Deep neural networks may have different functions when deployed in different wireless systems. We take modulation classifiers as an example, which is enough to illustrate the features of adversarial examples in wireless networks. In our settings, one central access point act as a transmitter, and distributed nodes work as receivers. Each node is equipped with a well-trained classification model, which helps determine the modulation type that the central access point uses to encode the signal. The adversary aims to disguise the waveform of the over-the-air radio signal and misguide the classifiers further to incur tremendous consequences.

We categorize the previous works according to consideration of the distinct channel effect and broadcast nature in the wireless system scenario.

3.1   Consideration of Channel Effect

Different from other domains, the effect of channels will weaken the power of adversarial examples, and even worse, disable them. To implement an adversarial example in the realistic wireless systems, attackers are supposed to take channel effect into account.

Channel-Ignorant Attack. In [13], a white-box adversarial example generation algorithm is proposed. The authors utilize the fast gradient methods (FGM) [3] to optimize the adversarial example. They formulate such an attack scenario. The adversary adds a small perturbation r_x at the receiver's position when the central transmitter sends a wireless signal x to the receiver, so the signal received will be $x_{adv} = x + r_x$. The target of the attack is to craft a tiny perturbation r_x so that it leads to victim model's misclassification. Moreover, they also utilize the method of principal component analysis (PCA) to fabricate universal adversarial perturbations (UAP), which they implement experiments to demonstrate its validity. The disadvantage of their work is that they ignored the intrinsic channel effect in the wireless scenario and they modify the input by directly adding a perturbation, which is impractical in the realistic environment.

Channel-Considered Attack. The attack methods of [2,5,13] all focus on how to efficiently generate more powerful perturbations with limited knowledge about the network. But they fail to take the distinct channel effect of wireless scenario into consideration, in which way, they can never ensure that the perturbations injected have enough power to function well. In [6], the authors first show that the works without consideration of channel effect fail in the real world. And then, they accomplish a channel-considered attack by adding one restriction of power budget P_{max} to the optimization problem, in which way, they can fabricate an adversarial perturbation with both high adversarial performance and high power efficiency.

3.2   Consideration of Multi-target Attack

Attackers should never neglect the fact that samples in wireless networks are not directly fed to the DNNs, but are broadcast to the shared channel. This adds more possibility to success in attacking multiple receivers simultaneously.

Receiver-Specific Attack. In the previous works [2,5,9,13], adversarial example generation algorithms have been demonstrated efficient when the attack is carried out strictly. The shortcoming of these attacks is that the crafted adversarial examples are specific to target receivers and inefficient when used to attack other receivers. That is because models deployed in the receivers have specific gradient information and channel information.

Broadcast Attack. Spoofing one receiver among the whole network can only lead to the breakdown of one node. Considering the broadcast characteristic of wireless communication, it is more devastating and viable to attack multiple receivers at the same time in the network. Nevertheless, the different intensities of the channel effect make it difficult to implement. In [6], the authors proposed two solutions. The first one is that we can separately attack each of the m receivers and obtain corresponding m adversarial examples. We can finally get a weighted sum as the ultimate adversarial example. The authors suggest that the weight of each node can be determined by line search algorithm. The second but more rational approach is to take advantage of a jointly calculated loss function. This loss function score aggregates all the information we need to attack multiple receivers simultaneously.

4   Adversarial Example Attack Countermeasures

Inspired by the defenses used in other domains, like CV and NLP, several strategies have been introduced to improve deep learning-based wireless system's robustness to adversarial examples.

4.1   Adversarial Train

Similar to other domains, adversarial training strategy can be used to defend against the threats of adversarial examples. During the training process, we can add adversarial examples correctly labeled to the training set as a data augmentation method, which can enhance models' classification ability to a certain extent. However, when faced with adversarial examples created through a different method, the model will still be successfully attacked. More generally, a method called randomized smoothing can improve the model's anti-interference ability against adversarial examples. More specific, we emulate adversarial examples by augmenting the training set with randomized noise, which a certified defense.

4.2   Random Transmission Error

Conscious of the existence of adversaries, the transmitter can add the uncertainty of the deep learning-based wireless network by randomly taking wrong transmission actions, such as transmitting in a busy channel or not transmitting in an idle channel. It helps fool the adversary with wrong channel information and obstruct the generation and implementation of adversarial examples. Inevitably, this method will lead to performance reduction, so it is vital to find an appropriate balance between network performance and security guarantee [14].

4.3   Statistics-Based Detection

Proposed by [18], the detection method is a two-step approach, which utilizes the peak-to-average-power ratio (PAPR) of the radio frequency samples and the softmax output of the classifier to effectively detect adversarial examples. PAPR is a widely adopted metric used in wireless communication researches to illustrate the modulation type. Therefore, if the modulation classifier outputs one modulation label and meanwhile the PAPR represents a different label, the input will be suspected as an adversarial example and more tests should be performed. During the second detection stage, the suspicious sample's softmax logits are used to analyze if there exists a distribution shift caused by adversarial example noise. In this way, the receiver can decide to accept or reject the sample to avoid being attacked.

5   Conclusion

As discussed above, deep neural networks employed in wireless networks are likely to suffer from adversarial example attacks, which incurs potential security risks in the real world. Meanwhile, there are some effective defense strategies that have been proposed to address the adversarial example attack threats. However, none of them can perfectly defend against all kinds of adversarial example attacks without reducing transmission quality. Moreover, we point out that the transmission features of wireless networks like open channels have not been taken full advantage of yet. Therefore, more efforts are in demand to put forward more aggressive attack schemes to find out the potential security risks hidden in wireless networks. It is also crucial to devise more robust models to invalidate adversarial example attacks while ensuring high quality of service.

References

1. Chakraborty, A., Alam, M., Dey, V., Chattopadhyay, A., Mukhopadhyay, D.: Adversarial attacks and defences: a survey. arXiv preprint arXiv:1810.00069 (2018)
2. Flowers, B., Buehrer, R.M., Headley, W.C.: Evaluating adversarial evasion attacks in the context of wireless communications. IEEE Trans. Inf. Forensics Secur. **15**, 1102–1113 (2019)

3. Goodfellow, I.J., Shlens, J., Szegedy, C.: Explaining and harnessing adversarial examples. arXiv preprint arXiv:1412.6572 (2014)

4. Huang, R., Xu, B., Schuurmans, D., Szepesvári, C.: Learning with a strong adversary. arXiv preprint arXiv:1511.03034 (2015)

5. Kim, B., Sagduyu, Y.E., Davaslioglu, K., Erpek, T., Ulukus, S.: Over-the-air adversarial attacks on deep learning based modulation classifier over wireless channels. In: 2020 54th Annual Conference on Information Sciences and Systems (CISS), pp. 1–6. IEEE (2020)

6. Kim, B., Sagduyu, Y.E., Davaslioglu, K., Erpek, T., Ulukus, S.: Channel-aware adversarial attacks against deep learning-based wireless signal classifiers. IEEE Trans. Wirel. Commun. (2021)

7. Kim, B., Sagduyu, Y.E., Erpek, T., Ulukus, S.: Adversarial attacks on deep learning based mmwave beam prediction in 5G and beyond. arXiv preprint arXiv:2103.13989 (2021)

8. Kim, B., Shi, Y., Sagduyu, Y.E., Erpek, T., Ulukus, S.: Adversarial attacks against deep learning based power control in wireless communications. arXiv preprint arXiv:2109.08139 (2021)

9. Kokalj-Filipovic, S., Miller, R., Morman, J.: Targeted adversarial examples against RF deep classifiers. In: Proceedings of the ACM Workshop on Wireless Security and Machine Learning, pp. 6–11 (2019)

10. Kurakin, A., Goodfellow, I., Bengio, S., et al.: Adversarial examples in the physical world (2016)

11. Nazir, R., Kumar, K., David, S., Ali, M., et al.: Survey on wireless network security. Archiv. Comput. Methods Eng. 1–20 (2021)

12. Papernot, N., McDaniel, P., Wu, X., Jha, S., Swami, A.: Distillation as a defense to adversarial perturbations against deep neural networks. In: 2016 IEEE symposium on security and privacy (SP), pp. 582–597. IEEE (2016)

13. Sadeghi, M., Larsson, E.G.: Adversarial attacks on deep-learning based radio signal classification. IEEE Wirel. Commun. Lett. 8(1), 213–216 (2018)

14. Sagduyu, Y.E., Shi, Y., Erpek, T.: IoT network security from the perspective of adversarial deep learning. In: 2019 16th Annual IEEE International Conference on Sensing, Communication, and Networking (SECON), pp. 1–9. IEEE (2019)

15. Sagduyu, Y.E., et al.: When wireless security meets machine learning: motivation, challenges, and research directions. arXiv preprint arXiv:2001.08883 (2020)

16. Yuan, X., He, P., Zhu, Q., Li, X.: Adversarial examples: attacks and defenses for deep learning. IEEE Trans. Neural Networks Learn. Syst. 30(9), 2805–2824 (2019)

17. Zhang, J., Li, C.: Adversarial examples: opportunities and challenges. IEEE Trans. Neural Networks Learn. Syst. 31(7), 2578–2593 (2019)

18. Kokalj-Filipovic, S., Miller, R., Vanhoy, G.: Adversarial examples in RF deep learning: detection and physical robustness. In: 2019 IEEE Global Conference on Signal and Information Processing (GlobalSIP), pp. 1–5. IEEE (2019)

Headmotion: Human-Machine Interaction Requires Only Your Head Movement

Duoteng Xu[1](✉), Peizhao Zhu[2], and Chuyu Zheng[3]

[1] College of Mechatronics and Control Engineering, Shenzhen University, Shenzhen 518061, Guangdong, China
2019112144@email.szu.edu.cn
[2] College of Computer Science and Software Engineering, Shenzhen University, Shenzhen 518061, Guangdong, China
[3] College of Electronics and Information Engineering, Shenzhen University, Shenzhen 518061, Guangdong, China

Abstract. With increasing demand for smart wearable devices and the booming development of pervasive computing, more and more new human-computer interaction methods for wearable devices are proposed to make up for the shortcomings of traditional wearable device interaction methods and improve the efficiency and ubiquity of interaction.

Up to now, the human-computer interaction of wearable devices is still dominated by contact interactions, such as touching the screen and pressing physical buttons. This interaction method is convenient in most scenarios, but there are limitations in some situations, such as disabled people cannot use their hands for human-computer interaction, and drivers are not suitable for touch interaction with their hands when driving. To address this shortcoming, we designed a natural interaction system for ear-worn smart devices, which includes a deep network recognition model based on acceleration, angular velocity and angle data of head motion collected by inertial units worn on the ear. The interaction system now can realize human-computer interaction of head motion in various complex scenarios, which greatly liberates the user's hands. We have experimentally verified the excellent accuracy and real-time performance of our designed system.

Keywords: Human-computer interaction · IMU · Android · Machine learning

1 Introduction

With the rapid development of information technology, more and more studies have begun to focus on human behavior identification and human-computer interaction, and strive to improve people's living standards through science and technology. At present, the ways to realize human-computer interaction are traditional interaction and new interaction. Among them, traditional interaction methods, such as keyboard interaction, touch screen interaction, have been widely used in our lives. However, traditional interaction will bring some inconvenience to people, such as keyboard, touch screen interaction

© ICST Institute for Computer Sciences, Social Informatics and Telecommunications Engineering 2022
Published by Springer Nature Switzerland AG 2022. All Rights Reserved
K. Wu et al. (Eds.): ICECI 2021, LNICST 437, pp. 98–107, 2022.
https://doi.org/10.1007/978-3-031-04231-7_9

requires the use of hands and eyes, voice interaction must be used in a quiet environment and easy to disturb others. Under the inconvenience brought by the traditional way of interaction, the new way of interaction arises at the historic moment.

Some researchers have devoted themselves to the interactive intelligence of existing wearable devices. Hui-Shyong Yeo [1] and others designed a smartwatch WatchMI. Users realize various functions of smartwatch by touching, twisting and translating smartwatch, such as music player, clock setting, map display, text input, control of remote devices and so on. To some extent, this interaction method solves the problem of thick fingers on the watch screen, and it is also widely used, but it still needs to use both hands to complete the interaction, so it is inconvenient to use.

Some researchers are devoted to the study of physiological signals, such as muscle sound signals (MMG), ECG signals (ECG) and so on. Tianming Zhao [2] proposed a gesture recognition system based on photoelectric volume pulse wave detection (PPG), which can use commercial wearable devices to recognize fine-grained gestures at the finger level. The system detects the blood flow of the wrist, and when the hand moves, the blood flow changes, so as to realize the hand movement detection. This kind of interaction does not need to use the eye to gaze at the screen, uses the hand to complete the motion detection. Obviously, the method of detecting activity through physiological signals is more natural than "virtual devices" and 'smart devices". On the other hand, due to the particularity of physiological signals, it is difficult to guarantee the accuracy of the system.

The design and implementation of the HeadMotion natural interaction system for ear-wearing intelligent devices can detect the user's head movement in real time and interact naturally in the case of freeing hands. This kind of interaction enables users to interact at will, and is suitable for a variety of scenarios, which will bring great convenience to people in use. Compared with other interactive methods, it can solve the problem that two hands can not be used to control the device in special cases, because the user can control the device by recognizing the head movement. At the same time, this interaction mode does not have high requirements for hardware, and any earwear device or head-mounted device with inertial measurement unit (IMU) can realize the system.

2   Hardware and Software Design of Equipment

2.1   Hardware Introduction

In order to make the collected data as close as possible to the actual product application scenario, we need to build the hardware platform of this system on the headset. However, the headphones sold in the market at this stage are highly integrated, which makes it difficult for us to carry out secondary development of software and hardware. To solve this problem, we independently developed a set of data acquisition devices that can support ear-worn. The design of hardware circuits and product shells take into account various factors such as versatility and resource consumption, and maximize the restoration of the user wearing the headset, making it easy to port to traditional headphones.

After several iterations of updates, the final version of the ear-worn device consists of a nine-axis IMU, a microcontroller ESP32, a 3.7 V Li-ion battery and 3D printed parts, whose PCB layout and 3D model diagram are shown in Fig. 1, and the final physical drawing is shown in Fig. 2. When the user's head moves, the IMU above the ear is simultaneously driven and collects signals of angular velocity, angle and linear acceleration in the X, Y and Z directions in the 3D coordinate system and transmits them to the microcontroller ESP32 via serial communication, for a total of $3 \times 3 = 9$ channels. The microcontroller ESP32, as the master chip, receives the signals measured by the IMU and transmits the data wirelessly to the Android application on the cell phone using the Bluetooth function that comes with the ESP32. In addition, the hardware platform is powered by a 3.7 v miniature lithium battery.

（a）diagram of printed circuit board   （b）2D model of printed circuit board   （c）3D model of printed circuit board

Fig. 1. Printed circuit board of hardware system

（a）Housing 3-D model of printed circuit board   （b）Physical picture of hardware

Fig. 2. Housing 3-D model of printed circuit board and Physical picture of hardware system

2.2 Hardware Programming

The embedded software is based on the Arduino platform, and is programmed on Arduino IDE using Champact + language. With the help of the rich open source function library in Arduino, it is convenient to complete the basic driver of each module, such as the library "JY901.h" which depends on IMU and the library "BluetoothSerial.h" of ESP32. UART reads IMU data, calculates Euler angle from quaternion, and Bluetooth sends head action data.

The nine-axis IMU JY901 we use includes an accelerometer, a gyroscope and a magnetometer, which can obtain the linear acceleration, angular velocity and magnetic field of the user's head movement. Because the data obtained by the gyroscope has white noise when measuring the angular velocity, the method of using the angular velocity to obtain the Euler angle directly will bring the integration error. Better results can be achieved by fusing all the original motion data through a stable filter. Therefore, we add Kalman filter to the hardware data acquisition program to obtain more accurate and stable data.

For head movement, posture is also an important feature to distinguish different head movements. Therefore, it is very important to get posture from the original data. The JY901 module we use has an integrated attitude solver, which can calculate the motion attitude more quickly and represent and output it in quaternion format. For hardware devices, both quaternion and Euler angle can be used to describe attitude, but Euler angle is closer to people's physical understanding of attitude and is more conducive to our subsequent data feature analysis, so we use the following formula (1) to convert the quaternion output of JY901 module into Euler angle on the hardware side [3].

$$
\begin{cases}
pitch = \arcsin[2(q_0 q_2 - q_1 q_3)] \\
roll = \arctan \frac{2(q_0 q_1 + q_2 q_3)}{q_0^2 - q_1^2 - q_2^2 + q_3^2} \\
yaw = \arctan \frac{2(q_1 q_2 + q_0 q_3)}{q_0^2 + q_1^2 - q_2^2 - q_3^2}
\end{cases}
\tag{1}
$$

where:

pitch—Pitch angle, range from $-90°$ to $90°$;

roll—Roll angle, range from $-180°$ to 180;

yaw—Heading range from $-180°$ to 180;

q_0, q_1, q_2, q_3—Quaternion.

3   Experimental Environment and Database Construction

This system requires subjects to wear our home-made hardware device to acquire inertial unit data during head movements to train the head movement classification model. For this purpose, we invited eight volunteers, aged between 20 and 24 years old, who were all students, to participate in the database building. Each subject completed a specified set of movements wearing our home-made hardware device, including twelve movements: head down, head down twice, head up, head up twice, head left lean, head right lean, head left turn, head right turn, head left turn twice, head right turn twice, head left turn then right turn, head right turn then left turn, and each movement was repeated 50 times. The data was numbered from P1 to P8 according to the subjects. In order to facilitate the presentation of the results, the twelve movements were numbered, and the corresponding numbers of each movement are shown in Fig. 3.

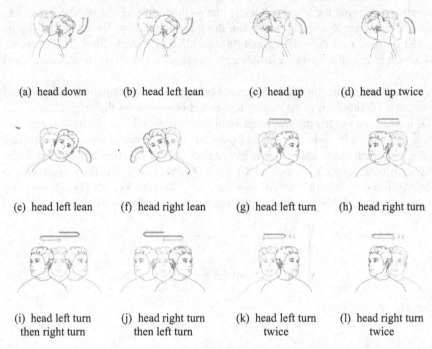

(a) head down   (b) head left lean   (c) head up   (d) head up twice

(e) head left lean   (f) head right lean   (g) head left turn   (h) head right turn

(i) head left turn
then right turn   (j) head right turn
then left turn   (k) head left turn
twice   (l) head right turn
twice

Fig. 3. Schematic diagram of head movement

4   Construction of the Human-Computer Interactive System

4.1   Overall Architecture of Interactive System

Figure 4 shows the overall block diagram of the system. The system is mainly divided into head posture data acquisition, data transmission, data visualization and preservation, model training, motion detection/segmentation, motion recognition, natural interaction and so on. Here we introduce the whole system through the training process and application process.

HeadMotion Training Process. Users wear ear-wearing smart devices for head movements. After the head movements are sensed by intelligent devices, the main control chip ESP32 reads the signals collected by IMU through UART, and then transmits the IMU signals to the mobile phone through its own Bluetooth controller. After receiving the data sent by Bluetooth, the Android application software on the mobile phone visualizes and saves the data, and establishes the data set needed for model training in the database. The PC side reads the data set, carries on the data preprocessing, the feature engineering, the training model, then derives the machine learning model, and finally deploys the machine learning model to the Android application software.

HeadMotion Application Process. When the user actually uses the earpiece smart device, the posture data flows to the mobile phone through the same process. At this time, the mobile phone can detect/segment the head movement in real time and recognize the head movement. The mobile phone will control the Map application to perform corresponding operations (such as map view movement and zoom, etc.) according to different head movements, and the response results of the Map application will be fed back to the user in real time, thus completing the whole process of natural interaction.

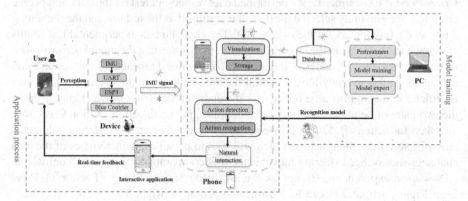

Fig. 4. The overall block diagram of the system

4.2   Construction of Recognition Model

The traditional convolution neural network has good performance in extracting the features of single frame signal, but it is poor in learning time series with a long time span. Yoshua Bengio pointed out in the reference that with the continuation of the time step, the current error messages will not affect the iterations with a long time span [4]. In view of this, Hochreiter and Schmidhuber proposed a special network, long-term and short-term memory network (Long short-term memory, LSTMs) [5], which introduces memory gate and forget gate on the basis of the traditional cyclic neural network, and determines when to remember or ignore the input in the hidden state through the special mechanism, so as to control the span of the cyclic neural network in the time-dependent relationship.

In order to learn the dependence of the time series data of head movements in the time dimension, so as to better classify the head movements, we choose the long short-term memory neural network to model the collected data. Considering the power consumption and efficiency, we finally choose the three-axis angular velocity time series data as the input of the network, which can achieve a very good classification effect.

4.3   Evaluation of Recognition Model

We conducted two sets of experiments on the data of 8 people collected.

Non-cross-Person Experiment. In this experiment, the data of each subject is trained and tested separately. Thanks to the strong learning ability of the LSTM network, it can achieve excellent performance in non-human experiments, and the classification results of non-human experiments are very excellent, basically reaching 100% classification accuracy.

Cross-Person Experiment. We performed a leave-one-out test on the data of 8 people collected. We randomly selected the data of one subject as the test set, and the remaining 7 bits as the training set for the experiment. The cross-human experimental test results are shown in Fig. 5. From the confusion matrix, we can see that the model performs well on the test set. Action A and action B, action H and action J repeat the same action again and again, so they already have a certain feature similarity in the original data, which is difficult to distinguish time periods for the endpoint detection model. Consequently, the two pairs of behaviors are easy to be confused in classification. Action C is easily mistaken for actions B, D and E. We suspect that this is because different volunteers have different movement habits, which will lead to personal characteristics of the data characteristics of head steering movements. It is comparatively easy to be confused in cross-person experiments. Except for the low recognition accuracy of action C (Head Lean Right), action D (Head Left Turn) and action H (Right Then Left), other head movements have been classified accurately.

Further modeling work is under way. Under the premise of controlling power consumption, we will further enhance the diversity of the input data of the identification model by merging the collected inertial group data and the calculated pose data.

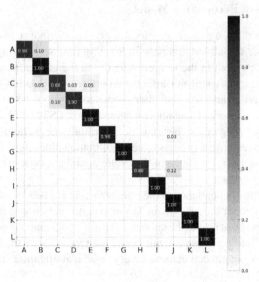

'Down': 'A', 'Down_Twice': 'B', 'Lean_Left': 'C', 'Lean_Right': 'D','Left': 'E','Left_Then_Right': 'F', 'Left_Twice': 'G', 'Right': 'H','Right_Then_Left': 'I','Right_Twice': 'J', 'Up': 'K', 'Up_Twice': 'L'

Fig. 5. Confusion matrix for twelve actions

4.4 Endpoint Detection in Real-Time Interactive System

Endpoint detection, also known as voice activity detection, is often used to intercept speech and non-speech segments in speech signals. In this system, in order to detect the head movement in real time, it is necessary to segment the data of each head action from the continuous data stream, so the endpoint detection technology in speech signal processing is applied to this system. Common endpoint detection methods include standard deviation detection, constant false alarm (CFAR) detection and so on.

- **Standard deviation detection.** The methods detect the beginning and end of the signal according to the real-time standard deviation of the signal. This method can achieve a good detection effect by adjusting the appropriate threshold in the case of constant noise [6]. However, it is not suitable to apply this method when the noise is unclear or the noise will change.
- **CFAR.** The methods can obtain noise according to the environment and obtain the threshold dynamically according to the noise, so as to detect the signal. The algorithm performs well under the condition of stable noise and is often used for signal detection in atmospheric noise and clutter [7]. The signal noise of this system comes from the signal with high sensitivity such as angular velocity. The sudden change caused by this kind of signal will affect the performance of CFAR, and the noise threshold is too large to detect the head movement.

This system adopts speech activity detection based on statistical model proposed by J. Sohn, N. S. Kim [8]. In this method, a robust speech activity detector for variable rate speech coding is developed, and the developed speech activity detector uses decision-oriented parameter estimation method for likelihood ratio test. In this method, the short-time Fourier transform (STFT) of the signal is calculated, and the noise spectrum is estimated from the noise using the minimum statistics, thus the endpoint detection is carried out. The performance of this system is better than the traditional methods such as standard deviation detection, peak detection, constant false early warning and so on.

5 Actual Interactive Application

Head movement-based interaction system to meet the needs of achieving various scenarios of interaction. We developed a companion Android application that implements the head motion contactless control of the map interface to verify that the designed interaction system is deployable and effective. The complete interaction system including the Android application is illustrated in Fig. 4, among which Baidu Map Android SDK is a set of application programming interfaces based on Android 4.0 and above devices. Developers can utilize the SDK to develop map applications for Android mobile devices. By calling the map SDK interface, developers can easily access Baidu Map services and data to build feature-rich and interactive map applications. The system integrates Baidu Map into Android application software. After the system detects and recognizes the user's head movements in real time, the application software will use the application program interface provided by Baidu Map to control the map instead of the user's hands, such as map view movement and zooming, to complete the process of natural interaction according to the head movement recognition result.

The correspondence between the user's head movements and Map application is shown in Fig. 6. When the system detects/recognizes the user's head movement, the application software simulates the user to slide the screen or click the zoom button to realize the change of map view according to the correspondence. Since the interaction process is dynamic, it is not convenient to display it statically, so only some results of the Map application view movement and zooming are shown in Fig. 7.

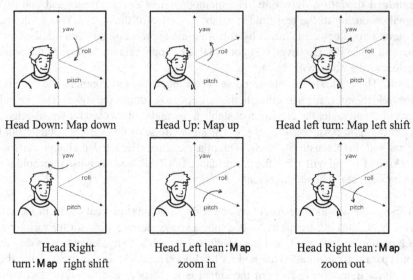

| Head Down: Map down | Head Up: Map up | Head left turn: Map left shift |

| Head Right turn: Map right shift | Head Left lean: Map zoom in | Head Right lean: Map zoom out |

Fig. 6. Correspondence between head movement and Map Android application

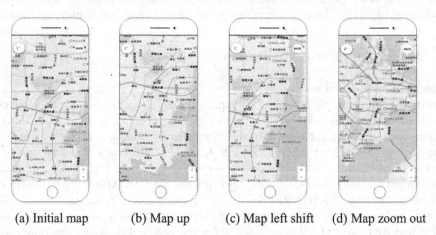

(a) Initial map   (b) Map up   (c) Map left shift   (d) Map zoom out

Fig. 7. Moving and zooming of the perspective of the Map Android application

6 Summary and Prospect

Under the background of the popularity of wireless headphones, artificial intelligence headphones will be the next development trend of headphones. HeadMotion's smart headwear device has the advantages of simple hardware, high integration and low cost, and can be easily integrated into headset products. The machine learning model deployed on the application software is simpler and faster than the deep learning model, and the accuracy in the real-time system reaches 87.3%, which meets the actual needs of users. In addition, the corresponding data training model can be collected according to the needs of users, so as to customize the action categories and achieve the customization effect. HeadMotion interacts naturally with application software, and developers can easily add or modify the corresponding interactive functions. For example, HeadMotion can help users control the movement and zoom of the view of the map with head posture, the start and pause of the music player, and the answer and hang-up of the phone when driving or cycling, making the driving and cycling process more safe and convenient. Not only that, HeadMotion can also help people with disabilities to use smart wheelchairs, so that users can control the movement of smart wheelchairs with head posture and reduce the burden on their hands. HeadMotion can be used in any scenario where two hands cannot be used or are not convenient to use. All in all, HeadMotion really enables natural interaction that frees users' hands.

References

1. Yeo, H.S., Lee, J., Bianchi, A., Quigley, A.: WatchMI: pressure touch, twist and pan gesture input on unmodified smartwatches. In: International Conference on Human-Computer Interaction with Mobile Devices and Services (MobileHCI), Florence, pp. 394–399 (2016)
2. Zhao, T., Liu, J., Wang, Y., Liu, H., Chen, Y.: PPG-based finger-level gesture recognition leveraging wearables. In: IEEE International Conference on Computer Communications (INFOCOM), Honolulu, pp. 1457–1465 (2018)
3. Zhang, F., Cao, X., Zou, J.: A new conversion algorithm between full-angle quaternion and Euler angle. J. Nanjing Univ. Sci. Technol. **26**(4) (2002)
4. Liang, J., Chai, Y., Yuan, H., et al.: Emotion analysis based on polarity transfer and LSTM recursive network. J. Chin. Inf. **29**(5), 152, 159 (2015)
5. Hochreiter, S., Schmidhuber, J.: Long short-term memory. Neural Comput. **9**(8), 1735–1780 (1997)
6. Yi, S., Qin, Z., Novak, E., Yin, Y., Li, Q.: GlassGesture: exploring head gesture interface of smart glasses. In: IEEE International Conference on Computer Communications (INFOCOM), San Francisco, pp. 1–9 (2016)
7. Yu, T., Jin, H., Nahrstedt, K.: WritingHacker: audio based eavesdropping of handwriting via mobile devices. In: Proceedings of the ACM International Conference on Ubiquitous Computing (UbiComp), Heidelberg, pp. 463–473 (2016)
8. Sohn, J., Kim, N.S., Sung, W.: A statistical model-based voice activity detection. IEEE Signal Process. Lett. **6**(1), 1–3 (1999)

Implementation of the Bone Grid Reconstruction Based on CT Data

Yicong Chen[(⊠)] [iD]

Shenzhen University, Shenzhen, China
chenyicong2018@email.szu.edu.cn

Abstract. Medical image processing has become an indispensable auxiliary means in the medical field, which make that the reconstruction of the internal image data of the human body can be visually presented to the doctor, providing the doctor with the simulation system of auxiliary diagnosis, which is helpful to find the lesions and improve the diagnostic accuracy. In this paper, a software system based on medical image data for the reconstruction of smooth three-dimension bone is studied. Firstly, software system read the medical image data to be processed (such as tumor site CT and MRI data), through the image denoising (remove bed information etc.), threshold processing (extract the interested region) and contour extraction (outer contour extraction), and other technical means to process medical image data of human surgical site, and then after processing of image data by three-dimensional reconstruction such as surface rendering mainly.

Keywords: Bed removing · Threshold processing · External contour extraction · Surface reconstruction

1 Introduction

The progress of contemporary medical science cannot be separated from medical auxiliary equipment and precision medical equipment. Since the last century, the invention of X-ray, CT, nuclear magnetic resonance, B-ultrasound and other imaging technologies have greatly promoted the progress of the medical industry, and the perfect combination of computer science and imaging technology expands the traditional sight, smell, inquiry and cutting treatment methods of doctors to personalized precision medicine assisted by "computer + imaging".

In the big data-driven world today, the use of computer graphics, image processing, data mining and other computer technologies to assist in analyzing medical information and image data has become an important development direction of contemporary medicine, and the development of computer graphics technology has deeply affected all aspects of our life. Among them, the application of 3D model is also more and more extensive, which has a significant impact in medical treatment, industrial manufacturing, games and other aspects. In the field of medicine, according to the patient's CT image or MRI (nuclear resonance) data before surgery, the 3D model reconstruction of the

© ICST Institute for Computer Sciences, Social Informatics and Telecommunications Engineering 2022
Published by Springer Nature Switzerland AG 2022. All Rights Reserved
K. Wu et al. (Eds.): ICECI 2021, LNICST 437, pp. 108–119, 2022.
https://doi.org/10.1007/978-3-031-04231-7_10

operation location is performed, which can allow the doctor to intuitively observe the three-dimensional structure of the operation position before the operation, to determine the actual medical condition of the patient, and to help doctors plan the surgical plan. Especially in complex surgery, it is conducive to improving the accuracy of surgery and providing the success rate of surgery.

The main idea of the 3D reconstruction process is to read the existing medical image data, divide the parts of interest and extract the edge contour, and then reconstruct the extracted 3D contour point gathering with a specific algorithm. Three-dimensional reconstruction is widely used in medical, film, games, virtual environment and other industries, such as three-3D digital cities, 3D maps, VR & AR games, medical 3D printing and other projects. The 3D reconstruction model is divided into face drawing models and body drawing models. Face drawing models can quickly render and retain grid data.

We targeted the CT image analysis for the reads and found noise in the original CT data, such as bed information, and we designed an information for the existing bone data to remove the noise bed from the original CT data. After removing the noise bed information, we segmented the regions of interest by thresholding, performed external contour extraction for the region of interest, and performed sequence contour smoothing processing.

2 Problem Analysis

2.1 Noise Processing

In the process of CT imaging, X-ray is generally used to scan the parts of the patient (such as bone), whereas the patient usually lies on the metal frame. In addition to scanning the information of the diagnostic site, the bed of a certain thickness is easily scanned as information as CT data, so the bed information belongs to the noise information (Fig. 1). When we segment the region of interest based on threshold segmentation, it is easy to interfere with subsequent operations in some cases. For example, in the figure above, we can find that the segmentation of the region of interest between the bed information and the brightness information of the area of interest (bone) threshold, the bed information as the area of interest, causing interference with the real bone information and causing errors.

In order to remove the effect of the bed as noise information on the segmentation region of interest, contour extraction, and the effect of 3D reconstruction, we need to remove the noise information of the bed from the raw data. By observing the sequence CT images, we can find that because the patient is lying on the metal bed during the CT scanning process, because the soft tissue information is between the human bone information and the bed information, and the soft tissue information is much lower compared to the bone information, there is a certain distance between the bed information and the bone information.

Among the existing bed-removing algorithms, with no bed-removing processing for specific bone CT data, this paper proposes an algorithm to remove noise bed information based on the intra-tissue connectivity of different tissues in CT images and the distance between bed and tissue. Due to the continuity of DICOM data, we know that the bed information exists in each CT figure, and the bed position always has a certain distance from the human bone, not continuous. Therefore, the average pixel value of the bed connected area must be higher than the average pixel value of the human area. It can be concluded that the connected area with a high average pixel value must be the regional information of the noise bed. In the next operation, the pixel value of the corresponding bed area can be set to 0 in the DICOM file of each layer, and the purpose of removing the bed can be achieved.

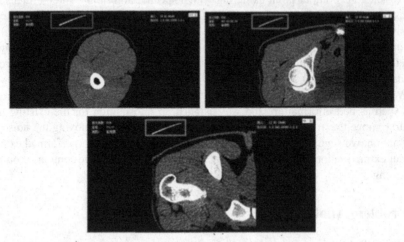

Fig. 1. The labeled bed information in three views of bone sections is the noise information that we need to remove.

The bed-removing algorithm process is: the first step, define a height * width size and initialize a total[height][width] pixel statistics array with each value of 0, then a height * width size and a mark [height][width] marker array with each value of 0 (A top view is a cross cut, the section of the body parallel to the ground, In the dataset processed here, an image of 512 * 512 in 446 layers, we get height 512 and width 512). In the second step, using algorithm 1, the distribution of 446 layer, i.e. for the image data of 446 layers, 8 threads (according to the X core of the computer, the distribution of the corresponding region, that is, for the image data of each layer 512 * 512, pass each pixel value, if the point (x, y) pixel 0 value is not 0, add t (total [x] [y] value, plus 1), instead of the real pixel value. If the real pixel value of the corresponding point is superimposed, when the pixel value of the area of interest is significantly greater than the information of the noise bed, it is easy to cause the average pixel value of the area of interest is too high after the later operation, and the area of interest is removed. The third step, using Algorithm 2, processing the marker array mark, if the pixel statistics array total [x][y] is not 0, the point (x, y) is the internal point in a connected area, the marker data corresponding to the marker value, mark [x] [y] is set to 255, otherwise the value of the marker array mark is not modified. In the fourth step, the mark array is judged on the connected region using the region growth method [10], and all the points corresponding to the Unicom region are recorded and the Unicom region is numbered and stored in the queue for secondary processing.

Finally, the average "pixel" value for each region can be counted based on the different connected regions already numbered, and on the previously acquired total pixel statistics array. Find out the connected area average pixel value is the noise bed information. After bed-removing, the raw data removes the bed information is Fig. 2.

Algorithm 1: (Statistical pixel distribution situation)

Input: I, total

Output: total

Step 1: Initializations. Define [m,n]=sizeof(I), total = zero[m,n]

Step 2: On the ith column and jth row in I ,for all pixels I (i,j), if we have I (i,j)>0, then total[i][j]+1

Algorithm 2: (Tagged array processing)

Input: total, I

Output: mark

Step 1: Initializations. Define [m,n]=sizeof(I), mark = zero[m,n]

Step 2: On the ith column and jth row in I ,for all pixels P(i,j), if we have P(i,j)>0, then total[i][j]=255

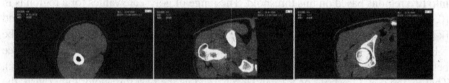

Fig. 2. The raw data after removing the bed information.

2.2 Partition of Regions of Interest

After removing the noise bed information, edge detection processing of the area of interest next requires the denoised image. Firstly, the area of interest after the denoised image is divided by the thresholding method, as shown in Fig. 3 below, the high luminance information is the bone information of interest; thereafter, the outer contour segmentation is performed according to the segmented region of interest.

Using the difference of interest between the image and other areas of interest, the image can be considered as a combination of two types of regions (regions of interest and non-areas of interest) with different levels of gray scale. Therefore, each image pixel is determined as belonging to an area of interest or a non-area of interest. In the data processing of this paper, we need to separate the muscle information and the bone information to extract the bone information of interest. And the yellow area in Fig. 6 is the extracted region of interest (bone).

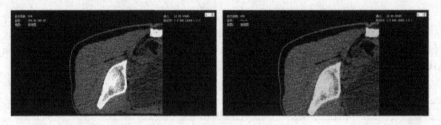

Fig. 3. High luminance information in the segmented image is the bone information of interest.

Common threshold processing is: global fixed threshold processing [10], adaptive threshold processing, and maximum inter-class difference threshold processing [11, 12]. Now compare the results of the three algorithms are as follows:

Fixed threshold method is to adopt a fixed threshold, without using the relevant algorithm to calculate this threshold, set by the program or the user. When a fixed threshold value is set, judge the pixel value of each point, if the pixel value does not belong to threshold value to 255, the pixel value is set to 0. This method requires the user to compare the effect of the different threshold setting on the threshold processing segmentation image, and finally obtain an optimal threshold.

Iterative adaptive thresholding method, using Algorithm 1, based on a fixed-threshold algorithm, First, given a fixed, reasonable threshold of K, The image can then be divided into two regions based on this threshold, The range of grayscale values for a region is in [0, K] and [k + 1, 255], Gray-scale levels were calculated separately at [0, Both k] and [k + 1, Mean pixel values V1 and V2 for 255], The new threshold was calculated to be K1 = 1/2 * (V1 + V2), Comparing the new thresholds of K1 and K, If the difference between the two thresholds is within the acceptable range a (which is given by the user), That is, the new threshold of K1 can be regarded as the best threshold; Otherwise, the new threshold was assigned to K, the images were redivided into two regions based on this threshold, and the average pixel values V1 and V2 of gray levels at [0, k] and [k + 1,255], respectively, until the new threshold K1 = 1/2 * (V1 + V2) and K were between the acceptance range a.

The maximum inter-class difference method, also known as Dashin method, proposed by Ozin in 1979, is considered the best algorithm for threshold selection in image segmentation, not affected by image contrast and brightness, and therefore has been widely used in image segmentation processing. The maximum inter-class difference method is to use the idea of clustering to divide the image's gray degree level into two parts according to the gray degree characteristics of the image, making the largest difference between the two gray degree levels, the smallest difference within each gray degree level, and the standard to measure this difference is the variance of the gray degree difference. When the variance between the two gray levels is, the difference between the gray level of the two parts is the largest, otherwise, when a part is misdivided into the other part, there must be a reduced difference between the gray level of the two parts, resulting in reduced variance, at which the maximum variance requirements are not met. Thus, the probability of error score is minimal when the gray scale variance of the two parts is greatest.

In summary, The global fixed threshold method is the artificial selection method, On the basis of analyzing the images, The interval where the threshold exists is determined, This method is of high reliability, But the efficiency is not desirable; However, the iterative adaptive threshold method has a great dependence on the selection of the current threshold estimates, It affects the number of iterations and the running time of the program; The maximum inter-class difference method is based on gray scale values, That is, the image is mainly the gray degree distribution, So it is also very sensitive to the noise information, And when the area of interest does not different from the non-region of interest, The gray scale value histogram presented as statistics has no significant bi-peaks, The separation of regions of interest was ineffective.

2.3 Contour Detection

After segmentation of the region of interest, contour edge detection of the region of interest is required. To reduce the model size during the 3D reconstruction, and to maintain the size of the model accuracy, we need to extract the outer outline of the region of interest before the surface drawing to obtain a 3D set of points of the outer outline, as input data for the 3D reconstruction in the next operation. After thresholding, binary plots of the region of interest can be obtained. Therefore, the obtained edges from our edge detection for the resulting binary graph can be viewed as profiles. Common ones are snake contour algorithm [13], LEVEL-SET algorithm [14], ant colony algorithm [15], GVF algorithm [16].

Here we use the Eight-Unicom Regional method. First, since points on an edge line are always adjacent up and right, a complete edge can be found by finding the eight-connected region of the edge. The 8 connection area of the point (x, y) refers to 8 points around this point, such as the 8 connection area of the point (x, y) is $(x - 1, y - 1)$, (x, y); $(x - 1, y)$; $(x - 1, y + 1)$; $(x, y - 1)$; $(x, y + 1)$; $(x + 1, y - 1)$; $(x + 1, y)$; $(x + 1, y + 1)$ if the central pixel (x, y) is 1, and at least one of the surrounding 8 pixels is 1. Eight-Unicom Regional method is as follows:

In the first step, for the profile extraction process of each image, a QList <QPoint> chain sheet object ContourList (which stores a set of values as a chain sheet and quickly indexes this set of data, also provides quick insertion and deletion operations) to store the set of profile edge points for each graph.

In the second step, using the edge detection algorithm 6, traverse each pixel of a given image, when a pixel is p (x, y), detect the pixel field p. If there is a point with a different pixel value in pixel field p, the point p can be judged as the boundary point and be added to the ContourList chain table, namely ContourList -> append (QPoint (x, y)).

In the third step, after going through a graph, that is, the set of contour points corresponding to the graph can be obtained, build a full black image of the same size as the original image (512 * 512 in this article), namely, all the pixel values of the initialized image are 0, and then traverse through all the points in the ContourList chain table and set the pixel value of the corresponding position of all points to 255 to obtain the contour image corresponding to the graph.

The fourth step, passing through the image sequence following the first three steps, has 446 binary plots in this dataset, that is, the point set of contour sequences, as shown in Fig. 4 below, which is the segmented outline.

Algorithm 3: (Tagged array processing)

Input: total, I

Output: mark

Step 1: Initializations. Define [m,n]=sizeof(I), mark = zero[m,n]

Step 2: On the ith column and jth row in I ,for all pixels P(i,j), if we have P(i,j)>0, then total[i][j]=255

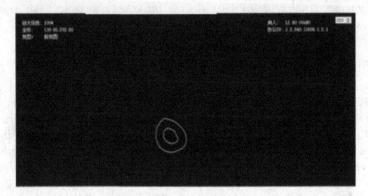

Fig. 4. Bone contour extraction by the Eight-Unicom Regional method.

Since the eight-Unicom region method is an extraction of all profiles in the image, including inner and outer contour, and cannot distinguish inner and outer contour, so that the external contour cannot be extracted, while in 3D reconstruction, generally only based on the external outline, the speed of the drawing and rendering of 3D reconstruction surface can be accelerated. Bountracing of binary image topology analysis can extract Chinese and foreign profiles. The boundary tracking [17] for binary image topology analysis was proposed by Suzuki S and Be K in 1985, which addresses the topological relations of digital binary images with two boundary following algorithms that can extract the surround relations between the boundaries of binary images.

The principle of this algorithm is: given a binary figure of a region of interest, first initialize the NBD to 1, indicating the serial number of the current boundary, using line by line scanning, each new scan, reset the LNBD to 1, for each pixel value is not 0, perform the following steps:

In the first step, scan line by line:

a. If the pixel value of the encountered point (i, j) is 1 and the point (i, j − 1) is 0, use this point as the outer boundary point after the outer boundary actual point, add the LNBD by 1, and save the point (i, j − 1) to (i2, j2)

b. If the pixel value of the encountered point (i, j) is greater than 1 and the point (i, j + 1) is 0, then (i, j) is the boundary point after the hole boundary starting point, the NBD increases 1, saves (i, j + 1) to (i2, j2), and the pixel value of the point (i, j) to the LNBD if the pixel value of the point (i, j) is greater than 1

c. If anything else, jump to step 4.

The second step, it determines the parent boundary of the current boundary based on the type of newly discovered boundary (outer or hole boundary) and the boundary with L N number LNBD.

In the third step, track the detected boundaries from the starting point (i, j) and perform steps from a to e:

a. From (i2, j2), detect pixels around (i, j) clockwise and find the first pixel value of not 0, the pixel value is assigned to (i1, j1), and if no pixel value of not 0 is found, (-NBD) is assigned to (i, j)
b. (i1, j1) is assigned to (i2, j2), and (i, j) to (i3, j3)
c. Start from the next element of the pixel point in the counterclockwise direction, check the nearby pixels of the current pixel point (i3, j3) counterclockwise, find a non-zero pixel value point, and let the first found point, assign the value to (i4, j4)
d. Change the value of the pixel point (i3, j3) as follows:
e. If the pixel value in the third step a) (i3, j3 + 1)) is 0, the-NBD is assigned to the pixel (i3, j3); if the pixel value (i3, j3 + 1) is not 0 and the value of the pixel (i3, j3) is 1, the value of the pixel (i3, j3) is NBD; otherwise, it does not change.

In the fourth step, if the value of the pixel point (i3, j3) is not 1, the absolute value of the value of the pixel point (i3, j3) is assigned to the LNBD, and the scan is continued with (i, j + 1) to know that the pixel reaches the last pixel, the bottom right corner. With the above four steps, the single contour of raw data can be extracted from the region of interest, as show in Fig. 5.

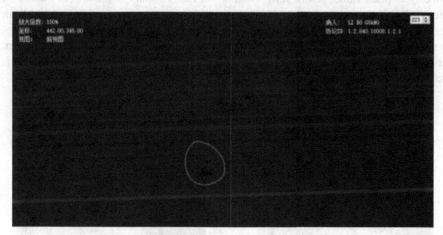

Fig. 5. The single contour extraction by the boundary tracking.

3   Experiment and Evaluation

In the threshold-based contour extraction of last section, in the threshold-based segmentation region of interest described above, the bone information and tissue information boundary information may be blurred in the CT data, and in the threshold processing, there is certain noise information, and these small noise information is not specially processed, which is easy to cause the model inaccuracy and smoothness in the subsequent 3-dimensional surface drawing process. For example, as shown in the figure below, the small red outline of Fig. 6(a) is the noise point. Therefore, in order to remove the error caused by the noise points presented above, we need to remove it from the sequence contour points.

In this paper, the morphological gradient denoising method is adopted. Using the morphological gradient [18, 19], the boundary or edge of the region of interest is located in the area of the gray scale of the image. The morphological gradient uses the combination of expansion and corrosion and the original image to enhance the intensity of the pixels in the field of structural elements, highlight the periphery of the highlight area, and provide higher quality data input for the contour extraction operation. First define a structural element, a matrix of a given pixel (generally square) with a central point in the structural element that align the pixels to be processed, and the processed results assign a value to the currently processed pixels.

The expansion operation is to overlap the central point of the structural element with the pixel point currently being processed, and then calculate the maximum value of the pixels in the original area covered by the structural element. This value is replaced with the current pixel value, to extend the binary image to the scope of the defined structural element and the same pixel value and the corresponding position of the structural element. The corrosion operation is to take the minimum value of the largest pixel in the corresponding area of the original image covered by the structural element, and replace the current pixel value, that is, some elements of the boundary of the area of interest of the original image can be removed, so that the binary image is reduced by a circle. With the diagram after the expansion operation process minus the corrosion operation process, the edge of the object can be highlighted to enhance the profile edge information. Small noise is eliminated, or the effect of smoothing the boundaries of larger objects is achieved, as shown in Fig. 6(b).

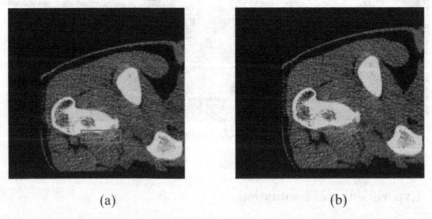

(a)   (b)

Fig. 6. There are relatively vague bone information and tissue information, as show in (a) and we show the denoised image information by morphological gradient denoising method in (b).

After removing some noise points of interest, by observing the set of sequence contour points, we found the presence of uneven contour. As shown in Fig. 7, the skeleton outline is obviously uneven, namely the partial absence of the contour point to deform the contour, and the profile needs to be smoothed.

This paper uses the adjacent layer contour smoothing idea, Sequence profile data obtained from observing edge detection, And the continuity of the CT sequence data, It can be found that without mutations (for example, the number of bone profiles increases or less), the profile data between the two adjacent layers have great structural similarity as well as the data correlation, like that, First by grouping the contour sequences, Given a large correlation between the contour sequences within each group, The contour sequences of the two adjacent groups are quite different (characterized by the number of profiles per each graph and the area surrounded by each contour, If a figure has more than 3 outlines, The area of the first three largest contours was chosen as the features); Then within each grouping, Try to add the profile data of the previous layer to the profile extraction of the image of the next layer as prior information, Data correlation of the two adjacent layers can be increased and smooth the contour edges; at the same time, Since the CT data are performed during the threshold segmentation process, Does not completely divide the area of interest (bone information), Therefore, the contour edges may not be smooth, When dealing with the current not slippery profile of the layer, The complete and smooth profile edges of adjacent layers can be added to the profile information to be processed, Can smooth the outline of the current layer, But it is also easy to attach adjacent layer-irrelevant information to the current layer.

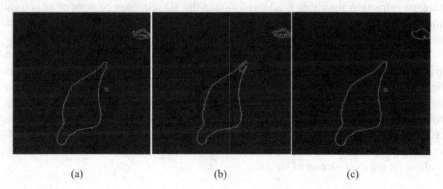

(a)   (b)   (c)

Fig. 7. (a) and (b) are the contour sequences of the two adjacent layers and (c) is new set of contour points processed by (a) and (b).

As shown in Fig. 7 above, (a) and (b) are the contour sequence of two adjacent layers, (b) is the set of contour points to be processed, and (c) is the new set obtained from the processing of adding the (a) figure information to the (b) figure. It is obvious that the unsmooth contour point set can be smoothed, but the irrelevant contour point set in the left figure can be easily added to the next layer.

4 Discussion

In this paper, after reading the sequence CT data, to avoid the sequence CT data in the sequence CT data, the original CT data is extracted from the area of interest in the image, the sequence 3D contour point set, 3D surface drawing, and subsequent smoothing processing and preservation.

In image preprocessing, in order to remove the effect of noise bed information on subsequent operations such as threshold segmentation, an algorithm for removing noise bed information is proposed based on the connectivity within the tissue and the distance between the tissue in the image.

In the threshold segmentation stage, comparing the three algorithms of global fixed threshold segmentation, iterative adaptive segmentation and maximum inter-class difference methods, we found that the global fixed threshold segmentation is better, but there are high requirements for users, and an in-depth understanding of the brightness information of medical images or the CT value of different tissues is needed.

During the contour extraction process, the contour is extracted by the Eight Unicom region method and found that all the contour information of the region of interest can be extracted, but the outer outline and internal outline are not clearly defined. Then according to the boundary tracking algorithm of the topology analysis of the binary image, the outer outline of the sequence outline can be extracted, and for some uneven phenomena of the external outline, the unsmooth contour based on the adjacent layer according to the continuity of the CT sequence image.

In the process of three-dimensional surface drawing process, the classic mobile cube isoplane extraction algorithm is adopted to map the 3D sequence contour point set, and smooth the smoothing grid with the idea of Laplace smoothing, mesh simplification and mesh refinement, making the reconstructed 3D grid relatively smooth.

Through the certain limitations of the above operation design, such as the reconstruction grid effect is not enough entity ideal, because the reconstruction is based on the extracted sequence contour point set, so the requirements for contour information is higher, and the segmentation of the area of interest may have certain error and uncontrollable noise phenomenon, the following work also needs to optimize the contour extraction algorithm. With the development of medical technology and computer graphics discovery, this kind of medical software can well assist doctors in the diagnosis, while reducing the risk rate of surgery.

References

1. Julesz, B.: A method of coding television signals based on edge detection. Bell Labs Tech. J. **38**(4), 1001–1020 (1959)
2. Roberts, L.G.: Machine perception of three-dimensional solids. Massachusetts Institute of Technology (1963)
3. Marr, D., Hildreth, E.: Theory of edge detection. Proc. R. Soc. London Ser. B Biol. Sci. **207**(1167), 187–217 (1980)
4. Canny, J.: A computational approach to edge detection. In: Readings in Computer Vision, pp. 184–203. Morgan Kaufmann (1987)

5. Deriche, R.: Using Canny's criteria to derive a recursively implemented optimal edge detector. Int. J. Comput. Vis. **1**(2), 167–187 (1987)
6. Bergholm, F.: Edge focusing. IEEE Trans. Pattern Anal. Mach. Intell. **6**, 726–741 (1987)
7. Rothwell, C.A., Mundy, J.L., Hoffman, W., et al.: Driving vision by topology. In: Proceedings of International Symposium on Computer Vision-ISCV, pp. 395-400. IEEE (1995)
8. Mildenberger, P., Eichelberg, M., Martin, E.: Introduction to the DICOM standard. Eur. Radiol. **12**(4), 920–927 (2001). https://doi.org/10.1007/s003300101100
9. Huang, Y., Ren, Y.: Image segmentation algorithm based on thresholding and regional growth method. Electron. Test (10), 23–25 + 36 (2012)
10. Bi, J.: Extraction method based on improved global threshold. Comput. Knowl. Technol. (12) (2013)
11. Bu, W., You, F., Li, Q., Wang, H., Duan, H.: An improved image segmentation method based on the Ozu method. Beijing Inst. Print. **23**(04), 76–78 + 82 (2015)
12. Lee, S.D., Xing, D.: Image block binarization algorithm based on Dajin method. (14) (2005)
13. Abd-Almageed, W., Smith, C.E., Ramadan, S.: Kernel snakes: non-parametric active contour models. Washington, DC, vol. 1, pp. 240–244 (2003)
14. Zheng, G., Wang, H.: A tree-like multiphase level set framework for 2-D and 3-D medical image segmentation. In: 2006 6th World Congress on Intelligent Control and Automation, Dalian, pp. 9645–9649 (2006)
15. Cheng, X.: Image segmentation method based on ant colony algorithm. University of Electronic Technology (2011)
16. Xu, C., Prince, J.L.: Gradient vector flow: a new external force for snakes. In: Proceedings of IEEE Computer Society Conference on Computer Vision and Pattern Recognition. IEEE (2002)
17. Suzuki, S., Be, K.: Topological structural analysis of digitized binary images by border following. Comput. Vis. Graph. Image Process. **30**(1), 32–46 (1985)
18. Yang, C., Li, X., Zhang, X.: Lip contour extraction of RGB-based improved region growing algorithm. In: IEEE International Conference on Software Engineering & Service Science. IEEE (2014)
19. Nath, R., Rahman, F.S., Nath, S., et al.: Lip contour extraction scheme using morphological reconstruction based segmentation. In: 2014 International Conference on Electrical Engineering and Information Communication Technology (ICEEICT). IEEE (2014)

Intelligent Vocal Training Assistant System

Yihong Li[✉] and Chengzhe Luo

College of Computer Science and Software Engineering, Shenzhen University, Shenzhen, China
1691135092@qq.com

Abstract. In professional vocal training, a way to evaluate the quality of vocalization is often needed. In order to solve various problems caused by the lack of professional instructors, a vocal training system for detecting the closed state of the vocal cords is proposed. We have proposed a robust vocal training system for the detection of the closed state of the vocal cords on the mobile terminal, which can analyze the closure of the vocal cords of the human body during vocalization, so as to evaluate the vocal cord ability without a professional teacher or professional equipment. In this system, we can use two wearable sensors, vibrating plate and headset, to collect the signals of the human vocal cords, or directly use the microphone of the mobile device to collect. And we use the convolutional neural network to analyze the signals and classify the closed state of the vocal cords. In order to build this system, we constructed a vowel data set classified by degree vocal cords closure, including the wearable sensors and mobile phone microphones we used. We compared the performance of the traditional vocalization pattern classification method and the convolutional neural network method we used to classify the vocal cord closure types on the data set we constructed and the public data set, and finally tested under two noise environments, and the preliminary results proved the usability of our system.

Keywords: Wearable devices · Vocal cord closed state detection · Convolutional neural network

1 Introduction

Traditional vocal music training generally requires one-to-one guidance from a professional teacher, and the place of teaching is also in a quiet and fixed place such as the piano room. The existing mobile vocal music system focuses on pitch and rhythm, almost no assessment of vocal quality, and cannot meet the basic vocal learning needs. If students do not focus on maintaining good sound quality at the beginning, they will develop wrong vocal habits, which will affect the sound effect and the health of the vocal cords.

In the quality of vocalization, the closed state of the vocal cords is a very basic indicator. In many vocal training theories, including EVT (Estill Voice Training), the vocal cords are divided into three basic states: normally closed, not tightly closed, and excessive closure. We use the terminology proposed by Sandberg to describe these three

© ICST Institute for Computer Sciences, Social Informatics and Telecommunications Engineering 2022
Published by Springer Nature Switzerland AG 2022. All Rights Reserved
K. Wu et al. (Eds.): ICECI 2021, LNICST 437, pp. 120–127, 2022.
https://doi.org/10.1007/978-3-031-04231-7_11

modes. The sound mode in which the vocal cords are not tightly closed is called breathy, because the sound is like the airflow noise during breathing. The sound mode in which the vocal cords are over-closed is called pressed, which means that the vocal cords are squeezed and over-closed and for normal vocal cords closed, it is called model.

Based on this, we have carried out research work on a vocal training system aimed at detecting the closed state of the vocal cords.

2 Related Work

The closed state of the vocal cord detection has always been a hot research issue in the field of vocal theory research. Its multi-faceted application value and academic value have caused extensive research by scholars and companies at home and abroad. It is mainly divided into the following research directions:

2.1 Detection of the Closed State of the Vocal Cords Based on Electroglottograph

The principle of detecting the closed state of the vocal cords based on the electroglotto-graph is to capture the bioelectric signals on the skin surface close to the vocal cords. The technique mentioned is to create a database consisting of sound booth recordings from participants, whom are required to sustain vowels (/a/, /e/, /i/, /o/, /u/) in their typical speaking voice at a comfortable pitch and loudness. Then, they are asked to produce the same vowel set again, while mimicking three non-modal voice qualities (Fig. 1).

Fig. 1. Electronic glottis

This method requires professional medical testing equipment, and has poor universality and no mobility, which cannot satisfy the need of general user.

2.2 Detection of the Closed State of the Vocal Cords Based on Accelerometer

It is a non-invasive attempt to indirectly measure the subglottal sound pressure, which can efficiently resist the external noise interference.

This method used a three axis acceleration sensor to press against the skin of neck to record the sensor signals. It identified a specific tissue around the larynx to access the subglottal pressure (Fig. 2).

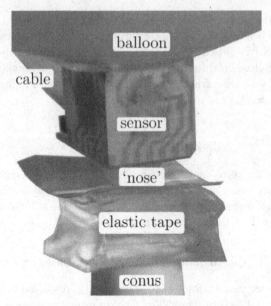

Fig. 2. Sensor in test environment-pressed on compressible elastic tape

On the other hand, this system requires user to firmly attach the accelerometer to their skin, which may cause skin discomfort. Furthermore, due to the low-resolution characteristics of the accelerometer itself, it is easily affected by body disturbances, which resulting in low recognition accuracy.

2.3 Detection of the Closed State of the Vocal Cords Based on Audio Signal Analysis

This method is a non-invasive detection method, and can be combined with existing commercial equipment (such as earphones, smart phones), and has universal applicability.

This detection method has a significant effect on distinguishing the voice type of voice and singing voice. Classification with support vector machine classifiers indicated that the proposed features and their combinations showed improved accuracy compared to usually employed glottal source features and mel-frequency cepstral coefficients (MFCCs).

However, the current technology can be divided into three categories: excessive closure, normal closure, and lax closure, and the accuracy of the results is greatly affected by changes in personnel, and also by changes in sound pitch, and they cannot achieve real-time detection.

2.4 Some Problems Existed in Related Research

The equipment is inconvenient to carry, and it is difficult to achieve real-time monitoring.

If user need to measure more accurate physiological signals, such as brain waves and electro-skin signals, you need to use large machines and oscilloscopes, which are difficult to carry at any time.

Some methods are inconvenient for people to actually use, and easily cause skin discomfort.

Some methods are based on accelerometers to detect the closed state of the vocal cords. But the accelerometer needs to be close to the skin close to the vocal cords, which will cause skin discomfort.

Monitoring results are not accurate enough.

Some low-resolution methods, such as accelerometers, may also be interfered by body motions, and the recognition accuracy is low. Moreover, the accuracy of the results is greatly affected by changes in personnel, as well as changes in voice pitch.

3   System Design

This system is an auxiliary vocal training system based on smart wearable devices. The overall design is based on skin vibration signals and sound sensing signals, it detects the closed state of the vocal cords when the user is speaking to guide the user's vocal learning in real time.

The provided system generally includes: a wearable vocal cord vibration sensor and a smart terminal, where the wearable vocal cord vibration sensor is used to collect skin vibration signals near the vocal cords and ear canal sound signals.

The wearable vocal cord vibration sensor includes an audio signal collector, a vibration signal collector, an audio processing module, a control unit, and a communication unit. The audio signal collector is used to collect the sound signal generated by the user's voice. The vibration signal collector is used to collect the skin at the position of the vocal cord. The skin vibration signal caused by the vibration. The audio processing module is used to process the collected sound signal and the skin vibration signal, and transmit it to the smart device via the communication unit. The control unit is used to coordinate the information interaction process between other modules or units, such as controlling the start and end of sound signal and skin vibration signal collection, and controlling the data transmission between the wearable vocal cord vibration sensor and the smart terminal. The smart device processes the received sound signal and skin vibration signal into a time-frequency graph, and inputs the pre-trained machine learning classifier to obtain the classification result of the closed state of the vocal cords (Fig. 3).

The following takes a smart phone with an Android operating system as an example to illustrate the detection process of the closed state of the vocal cords, including the following steps:

Start the smart vocal cord vibration sensor, the ear canal microphone collects the sound of the user's ear canal, and the original vibration signal of the skin near the vocal cord of the piezoelectric ceramic sheet. Filter and amplify the original vibration signal through the band-pass filter amplifying circuit of the intelligent vocal cord vibration sensor. The collected ear canal sound signal and the amplified and filtered vibration signal are transmitted to the mobile terminal in real time through the communication unit.

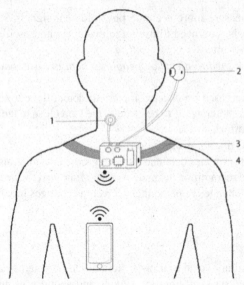

Fig. 3. An in-ear microphone[1]; A piezoelectric ceramic sheet[2]; An adjustable neckband[3]; A type-c charging port[4].

The mobile terminal performs processing on the received sound data and vibration signal data, and obtains the judgment result of the closed state of the vocal cords and vocal practice suggestions, and displays them in the APP. Finally, feed the result back to the user, and generate a related report.

Particularly, we design a system to analyze the sound data and vibration data. The step specifically includes the following steps:

The original ear canal sound data and skin vibration signal data are divided into frames, and divided into multiple windows for processing. First, the amplified and filtered skin vibration signal and the ear canal sound signal collected by the microphone are received, and the signal is divided into windows to process the data of each window.

Use a voice time detection algorithm (VAD) to detect voice data, and extract a data frame corresponding to the user's voice.

Convert the data frame into a time-frequency image through a short-time Fourier transform (SFFT). Specifically, the incoming data stream is buffered, the buffered data is retrieved after accumulation for a certain period of time, and both the sound data and the skin vibration signal data are converted into a time-frequency map through a short-time Fourier transform algorithm.

Through machine learning, the deep learning model analyzes the time-frequency image to recognize the closed state of the vocal cords.

4   Data Set

We invited 20 students major in vocal performance to assist us in the collection of data sets. In the process of collecting data, the students were asked to make sounds with different vocal cords closed by referring to the sample audio in a natural or simulated state (Fig. 4).

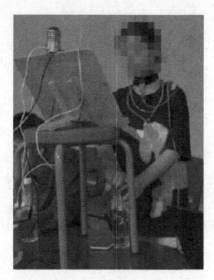

Fig. 4. Students in test

We asked the students to try a combination of 4 sounding scenes and 3 types of vocal cord closure situations. The 4 sounding scenes includes long vowel, short vowel, staccato[1], and fade.[2] The 3 types of vocal cord closure situations had been mentioned above, which are breathy, neutral, and press. We use a variety of data-collecting devices: mobile phone microphones, in-ear microphone, piezoelectric ceramic, and high-fidelity microphone.

5   Experiment and Result

After collecting the data, we use the current convolutional neural network model for feature extraction. After trying various convolutional neural network models, we got the following results.

The graph depicts that resnet18 method performs better than other methods and reach a considerable performance (Fig. 5).

On this basis, we tried to use different equipment to compare the better-performing methods in machine learning with resnet18 for cross-person[3] and non-cross-person experiments (Figs. 6 and 7).

---

[1] Tone changing sound.

[2] Volume changing sound.

[3] Non-cross-person refers to the mixture of all people's data, and then divides the training set and test set in proportion. Cross-person refers to the test on one person's data alone, and the data of other people is used to train the model.

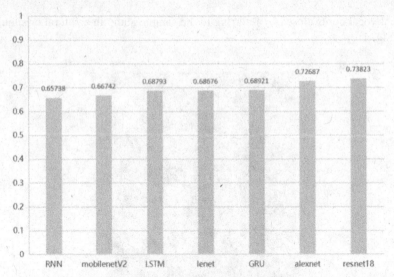

Fig. 5. Different performance of multiple Convolutional Neural Network models

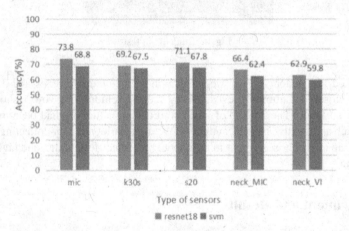

Fig. 6. Experimental results of different devices without cross-person

As is demonstrated in the graph, resnet18 is better in performance than traditional machine learning methods in many places.

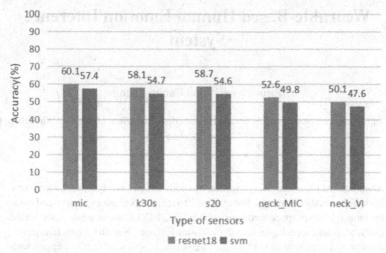

Fig. 7. Experimental results of different devices with cross-person

6   Conclusion

We propose a robust vocal music training system for vocal cord closure detection at the mobile end, which can analyze the vocal cord closure of human body when speaking. After comparing a variety of convolutional neural network models with traditional machine learning methods, we find that resnet18 has better performance. The accuracy of the test on the headset and vibrator is significantly lower than that of other devices. The possible reason for this phenomenon is the deviation of the data quality collected by the two sensors, such as the inherent noise of the hardware and the lack of high-frequency information. To solve this problem, we will improve the existing hardware equipment to improve the quality of collected data and improve the performance of the system.

References

1. Sundberg, J. The Science of the Singing Voice. Illinois University Press (1987)
2. Murphy, P.J.: Temporal measures of the initial phase of vocal fold opening across different phonation types. In: Models and Analysis of Vocal Emissions for Biomedical Applications: 6th International workshop, 14–16 December 2009, Firenze, Italy. Proceedings e report, p. 54. Firenze University Press, Firenze (2009)
3. Wokurek, W., Pützer, M.: Accelleration sensor measurements of subglottal sound pressure for modal and breathy phonation quality. In: Models and Analysis of Vocal Emissions for Biomedical Applications: 6th International Workshop, 14–16 December 2009, Firenze, Italy. Proceedings e report, p. 54. Firenze University Press, Firenze (2009)
4. Kadiri, S.R., Alku, P.: Mel-frequency cepstral coefficients of voice source waveforms for classification of phonation types in speech. In: Interspeech (2019)
5. Kadiri, S.R., Alku, P., Yegnanarayana, B.: Analysis and classification of phonation types in speech and singing voice. Speech Commun. **118**, 33–47 (2020)

Wearable-Based Human Emotion Inference System

Zirui Zhao[✉] and Canlin Zheng

College of Computer Science and Software Engineering, Shenzhen University, Shenzhen, China
2362534742@qq.com

Abstract. Many emotion recognition methods which have been proposed today have different shortcomings. For example, some methods use expensive and cumbersome special-purpose hardware, such as EEG/ECG helmets, while others based on cameras and speech caused risk of privacy leakage. With the prosperous development and popularization of wearable devices, people tend to be equipped with multiple smart devices, which provides potential opportunities for lightweight emotional perception. Based on this, we take actions on developing universal portable system and multi-source wearable sensing technology devices.

This paper designs an emotion recognition framework called MW-Emotion (Multi-source Wearable emotion recognition) featuring on low cost, universality, and portable commercial wearable devices to perceive multi-source sensing data and implement a system. It takes four basic emotions as the research object and implement an emotion recognition to explore deep context innovatively. The experimental results show that MW-Emotion has a recognition accuracy of 85.1% for person-dependent mode. The framework uses the method that different types of data are effectively fused through signal processing. We call it multimodal data fusion technology, which reduces the energy waste caused by data redundancy and effectively resists interference.

Keywords: Wearable devices · Emotion recognition · Multimodal data · Multiple perception

1 Introduction

Nowadays, the fast-paced life has brought increasing psychological pressure to modern humans. More and more people have symptoms such as emotional instability and long-term depression, and even suffer from psychological diseases such as anxiety and depression. According to Report on National Mental Health Development in China [11] from 2019 to 2020 released in March 2021, the results show that up to 31.1% of college students have depression or anxiety tendencies. The report points out that China's national mental health counseling services are in short supply and there is a big gap in service level. In the choice of psychological service methods, more than half of people tend to choose "self-regulation". The first step of self-regulation is to know your emotional state in time. To solve these problems, in recent years, researchers capture emotions

© ICST Institute for Computer Sciences, Social Informatics and Telecommunications Engineering 2022
Published by Springer Nature Switzerland AG 2022. All Rights Reserved
K. Wu et al. (Eds.): ICECI 2021, LNICST 437, pp. 128–135, 2022.
https://doi.org/10.1007/978-3-031-04231-7_12

through various techniques, such as capturing facial expressions, body postures, walking gait, and other limb body language of the human trunk for emotional inference, using microphones to record voice to extract semantic information or speech prosody information, and physiological signals, like Electroardioram (ECG), Electroencephalogram (EEG), Galvanic Skin Response apparatus (GSR) *etc*. However, these methods have the risk of privacy disclosure, and need to wear expensive and bulky professional sensor equipment.

To overcome these shortcomings, wearable devices have gradually become popular and diversified, and modern people even use a variety of wearable devices at the same time. Commercial wearable devices have gradually improved in terms of capacity, performance, and intelligence, providing new possibilities and huge opportunities for reliable and lightweight emotional exploration. Wearable devices are embedded with many physical sensors. These body language sensors can detect the user's movement, monitor physiological signals, and capture images, sounds, and videos. With the further development of the identification, including sensor technology and artificial intelligence technology, and with the help of low-cost commercial portable wearable devices, not only can physical data such as the user's heartbeat, steps, and gestures be obtained, it can also make deep Hierarchical emotional calculations possible. Different types of multi-modal emotional related data can be collected in an unobtrusive manner at the same time, which greatly enhances the portability and ease of use for users. To sum up, compared with previous related work, this new emotion recognition method based on low-cost, universal and portable wearable device perception data has the following three outstanding advantages: Equipment universality, Privacy security and Emotional validity.

2 Related Work

Emotion recognition has always been a hot research issue in the field of artificial intelligence. Its multi-faceted application value and academic value have caused extensive research by scholars and companies at home and abroad.

Body Language. Body language is a basic type of human social behavior. It is an important indicator of a person's emotions and inner state. It contains different types of non-verbal expressions, such as facial expressions, eye movements, body posture, walk gait, *etc*. However, this method has the following shortcomings: (1) expensive and requires huge calculations; (2) easy to cause privacy leakage; (3) The problem of emotion hiding (4) requires continuously track.

Speech Signals. There are two aspects. One is based on the acoustic characteristics of speech and the other is based on the semantic content of speech, features in the speech signal such as frequency spectrum, Mel cepstrum coefficient (MFCC), *etc*., and makes emotional judgment by analyzing the polarity of emotional characteristic words. However, there is a risk of leaking the content of the user's voice, and it is greatly affected by the difference in the habits of individual expressing emotions. It is also easy to pretend that the true internal emotions cannot be measured.

Physiological Signals. Common physiological signals for emotion recognition embraces EEG, ECG, GSR, Radar Signal Processor (RSP), *etc.* These physiological signals are more related to people's internal emotional state, but they are too complicated and bulky to carry (Figs. 1 and 2).

 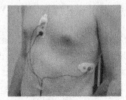

Fig. 1. EMG sensor applied to the jaw and ECG sensor applied to chest [1, 6].

Fig. 2. Respiration sensor and Skin conductivity, temperature and Finger blood volume pulse (BVP) sensor [1, 6].

Usage Pattern Perception. This emotion recognition method mainly analyzes and models the usage of sensors such as accelerometers, gyroscopes, microphones, GPS, light sensors, compasses, screen pressure sensors, and various applications in the mobile terminal to perform emotion recognition. However, the accuracy and reliability of this method still need to be improved.

Multimodal Perceptual Signals. The method is better and comprehensive than previous methods by integrating two or more different signals of the above technologies, and uses the information obtained from multiple modalities to cooperate to improve the performance of the model. Different modalities can be expressed in different sources or forms of information, such as sound modalities, image modalities, text modalities, EEG, EMG, ECG, and other domain modalities. People live in such an environment where multiple modes blend with each other, and integrate with what the machine hears, sees, hears, and feels, to give the machine and model better performance. Although this method of synthesizing multimodal sensing signals has the advantages of accuracy, it also has their disadvantages.

3   System Design

In this experiment, we use Multimodal Perceptual Signals as our experimental signals, then we design a system called MW-Emotion to sense the emotions and process them.

3.1 Multi-modal Sensing Signal Design

Compared with the above related work, the advantage of MW-Emotion system is that it can be non-invasive and portable to sense human emotions. The cost of the whole system is much lower than professional emotion sensing devices. It only needs headphones, watches, and smart glasses. What's more, it can be carried around and tested for a long time. More specifically, the MW emotion sensing system uses five mainstream portable micro wearable intelligent data sensing devices to collect multi-source and multi-modal data. These five devices are smart wristbands, smart headphones, smart glasses, smart necklaces and smart phones, which are worn on the user's head, ears, wrist, neck and nose. These conventional low-cost sensors on these intelligent devices, including microphone sensor and optical capacitance pulse sensor PPG, are used to collect the user's pulse signal and body sound signal respectively. The body sound signals include heart beating sound, nasal breathing sound, laryngeal trachea sound and other body sound signals. After sensing the data acquisition, the collected signals are integrated and sent to the mobile terminal in the form of data frames for processing. The mobile terminal further automatically and in real time infers emotions.

The wearing position and perceived data type are as follows. There are 5 main positions. Position 1 is an in-ear headset with a built-in micro microphone. When wearing, it forms a resonant cavity with the ear canal to amplify the sound of heartbeat; Positions 2 and 3 are microphones, which are respectively used to collect the tracheal sound and nasal sound of the throat. Breathing sound, tracheal sound and other body non speech sounds can be captured by these two microphone sensors. Positions 4 and 5 are optical capacitance pulse sensors, which can monitor the wearer's heartbeat. These physiological signals are closely related to human emotion and have the potential to reflect emotion.

At present, many researchers have explored and proved the correlation between respiration, heartbeat and other body sound signals and emotion from a biological point of view. For example, Ikuo Homma [3], a Japanese physiologist, discussed the relationship between breathing and emotion from the perspective of brain neurology, and pointed out that autonomous breathing is not only controlled by metabolic needs, but also constantly responds to emotional changes.

3.2 Multi-modal Signal Preprocessing

After collecting the multi-modal original signal, we first subtract the average value of each channel signal to remove the DC drift. In addition, due to the interference of nearby power lines, the power supply is 50 Hz AC current, so the collected signal contains 50 Hz component and corresponding odd harmonics. Nevertheless, there is obvious power frequency interference here. To reduce this, we first FFT the signals of each channel, set the corresponding coefficients of these interference components to zero, more specifically, use the suppression bands of [49,51] Hz, [149152] Hz and [249251] Hz to cut off the frequencies of the five channels, and then use the inverse fast Fourier transform (IFFT) to transform the signal back into a time domain signal sequence.

Preprocessing for Different Signals: For the five signals, different signal processing methods are adopted due to different signal types and acquisition positions. The following five locations are the five positions described above.

- Location 1: Since the main frequency of heartbeat signal is in [1, 6] Hz, we filter this channel using band-pass FIR filter with [0.1, 10] Hz to ensure information redundancy.
- Location 2/3: The throat and nose channels mainly detect breathing information, including the respiratory rate and depth. They also record non-speech body sounds such as laughter and crying.
- Location 4/5: For PPG signals, we first filter it with [0.1,10] Hz band-pass FIR filter. However, the PPG signals are affected by sensor and skin contact and whether sweating. Long time experiments lead to signal stability and low-frequency drifts. To eliminate such interference, we directly band stop the components less than 0.5 Hz after FFT transform, and then recover the signal through IFFT.

Normalization: Due to variations in quantization standards for different signals, normalization is necessary. Each channel signal is soft-normalized using the 5th and 95th quantiles.

3.3   Experiment Setup

In the experiment, we invited 30 users to participate in data collection, and used video or audio materials with different emotional colors to stimulate users' emotions. To get enough data, we let users self report their emotions during this period after observing each stimulus material.

3.4   Emotion Recognition Model

After the above steps, we use DenseNet as the recognition model. To improve its classification ability, we make full use of each layer of information. We use short-time Fourier transform (STFT) to convert each channel signal into time-frequency spectrum, and then feed them into the model.

STFT: The short-time Fourier transform (STFT) is to select a time-frequency localized window function, assuming that the analysis window function g(t) is stationary (pseudo stationary) in a short time interval. Move the window function so that f(t)g(t) is a stationary signal in different finite time widths, so as to calculate the power spectrum at different times. It uses a fixed window function. Once the window function is determined, its shape will not change, and the resolution of the short-time Fourier transform will be determined. STFT is a good choice for analyzing piecewise stationary signals or nearly stationary signals.

DenseNet121 Model: A milestone in the history of CNN is the emergence of ResNet model. ResNet can train deeper CNN models in higher accuracy using "skip connection". DenseNet achieves better performance than ResNet with fewer parameters and computational costs. The core of DenseNet model is to establish "dense connection" between all front layers. Another superiority of DenseNet is achieving feature reuse through connections between features on the channel.

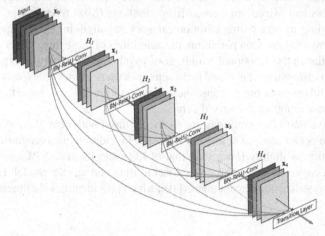

Fig. 3. A 5-layer dense block with a growth rate of k = 4. Each layer takes all preceding feature-maps as input [9].

For a L layer network, DenseNet contains $\frac{L(L+1)}{2}$ connections, which is a dense connection compared with ResNet. All previous layers are connected as input:

$$x_l = H_l([x_0, x_1, ..., x_{l-1}]) \tag{1}$$

Among them, the above $H_L(\cdot)$ represents non-linear transformation. It is a combined operation, which may include a series of BN, ReLU, Pooling and Conv operations. There may be multiple convolution layers between the L layer and the $L - 1$ layer.

DenseNet have many advantages. Due to the dense connection mode, DenseNet improves the gradient back propagation, making the network easier to train; It also realizes short-circuit connection through concat feature, realizes feature reuse, and adopts a smaller growth rate. The Characteristic Map of each layer is smaller, and the implicit "deep supervision" is realized.

4 Experiment

In our experiment, we used four public emotional stimulation data sets, namely Stim Film [4], EMDB [5], IADS [2] and SEED [7], which included video and audio widely used to induce specific types of emotions in psychological experiments to collect users' emotions. The data are collected by five wearable devices on different locations as shown in Fig. 3.

4.1 Results and Evaluation

We have tested DenseNet's learning model. Figure 4 shows the confusion matrix of the DenseNet implementation.

We used four basic emotions in the psychological sense, including Happiness, Neutrality, Sadness and Mixed emotions. Mixed emotions (Mix) refer to fear, nausea and anger. According to the existing emotion category paradigm in psychology, especially the two-dimensional emotion paradigm, the definitions of these three kinds of emotions are very similar in the emotional paradigm of psychology. During the experiment, by asking the experimenters, it is found that sometimes users cannot effectively distinguish these three kinds of emotions, because these three emotions often occur at the same time. Therefore, these emotions are mixed here.

We observe that other emotions are easily confused with neutrality, which may be caused by the actual aroused emotional intensity. In addition, the recognition accuracy of MW emotion is slightly lower than that of EQ radio [8] (*i.e.*, 87%), and EQ radio uses the data collected from the same subject to train and test the model. However, its performance is still better than memento [10], which [10] identifies six fitness types with an accuracy of 57%.

Fig. 4. The confusion matrix achieved by the DenseNet

Under the current setting, MW emotion can still achieve considerable recognition performance.

5   Conclusion

We propose a new low-cost, popular, and portable multi-mode wearable emotion recognition system, called MW emotion. The system can recognize emotional states in order to protect privacy, reliable detection and easy to use in daily life. Our experiments show that MW emotion can use multi-mode wearable devices to identify four basic emotional states with high precision, thus showing the potential in the future, that is, using low-cost, popular and portable wearable devices can perceive everyone's emotions.

This study reveals the potential correlation between shallow data and deep data perceived by low-cost, universal and portable wearable devices. It is a novel emotion inference technology and a new exploration to realize the perceptual interaction between machines and people. Its novelty is that it can noninvasively detect the potential relationship between emotion and more hidden and imperceptible physiological activities (such as breathing, heartbeat and other types of body sound). We handle these by designing appropriate data quality enhancement techniques and deep learning network, and we conduct real-world experiments to evaluate MW-Emotion and proves its favorable performance. To the best of our knowledge, MW-Emotion is the first work to demonstrate the feasibility to recognize emotion state using low-cost, pervasive and portable wearable devices.

With the increasing development of wearable devices, emotion recognition will serve people in a reliable, lightweight and simple way in the future. This technology has broad application prospects, such as intelligent recommendation based on emotional state, timely and continuous monitoring of emotion and emotional relief.

References

1. Haag, A., Goronzy, S., Schaich, P., Williams, J.: Emotion recognition using bio-sensors: first steps towards an automatic system. In: André, E., Dybkjær, L., Minker, W., Heisterkamp, P. (eds.) ADS 2004. LNCS (LNAI), vol. 3068, pp. 36–48. Springer, Heidelberg (2004). https://doi.org/10.1007/978-3-540-24842-2_4
2. Bradley, M.M., Lang, P.J.: The International Affective Digitized Sounds (IADS-2): Affective ratings of sounds and instruction manual. University of Florida, Gainesville, FL, Technical report B-3 (2007)
3. Homma, I., Masaoka, Y.: Breathing rhythms and emotions. Exp. Physiol. **93**(9), 1011–1021 (2008)
4. Schaefer, A., Nils, F., Sanchez, X., Philippot, P.: Assessing the effectiveness of a large database of emotion-eliciting films: a new tool for emotion researchers. Cogn. Emot. **24**(7), 1153–1172 (2010)
5. Carvalho, S., Leite, J., Galdo-Álvarez, S., Gonçalves, O.F.: The Emotional Movie Database (EMDB): A self-report and psychophysiological study. Appl. Psychophysiol. Biofeedback **37**(4), 279–294 (2012). https://doi.org/10.1007/s10484-012-9201-6
6. Koelstra, S., et al.: Deap: a database for emotion analysis; using physiological signals. IEEE Trans. Affective Comput. **3**(1), 18–31 (2011)
7. Duan, R.N., Zhu, J.Y., Lu, B.L.: Differential entropy feature for EEG-based emotion classification. In: 2013 6th International IEEE/EMBS Conference on Neural Engineering (NER), pp. 81–84. IEEE (2013)
8. Zhao, M., Adib, F., Katabi, D.: Emotion recognition using wireless signals. In: Proceedings of the 22nd Annual International Conference on Mobile Computing and Networking, pp. 95–108 (2016)
9. Huang, G., Liu, Z., Pleiss, G., Van Der Maaten, L., Weinberger, K.: Convolutional networks with dense connectivity. IEEE Trans. Pattern Anal. Mach. Intell. (2019)
10. Jiang, S., Li, Z., Zhou, P., Li, M.: Memento: an emotion-driven lifelogging system with wearables. ACM Trans. Sens. Netw. (TOSN) **15**(1), 1–23 (2019)
11. Zhang, X., Lewis, S., Firth, J., Chen, X., Bucci, S.: Digital mental health in China: a systematic review. Psychol. Med. 1–19 (2021)

Author Index

Printed in the United States
by Baker & Taylor Publisher Services